The Great Commanders
Rommel

W. Wessel
1942

Rommel

Charles Douglas-Home

EXCALIBUR

Designed and produced for
George Weidenfeld and
Nicolson Limited
London

ISBN: 0-525-701044
Library of Congress number
73-75720
Printed in Japan

Contents

Acknowledgements

The author and publishers wish to thank Manfred Rommel,
Frau Wilhelm Wessel, Dr Stephen Inwood and the
Imperial War Museum for their kind assistance and
co-operation in the preparation of this book. We would also
like to thank William Collins and Sons Limited, London,
for their kind permission to quote from *The Rommel Papers*,
edited by B. H. Liddell Hart, 1953; and The Office of
Alien Property, Justice Department, Washington, for
extracts from Rommel's *Infantry Attacks*, translated by
G. E. Kiddé, 1944. Pictures were researched by Sandra
Bance and maps researched and drawn by Richard Natkiel.
We are grateful to the many official bodies, institutions and
individuals for their assistance in supplying original
illustration material.

Introduction

IT IS APPROPRIATE that the first contribution to this series of the lives of Great Commanders should be concerned with a soldier who displayed most of the qualities and many of the defects of the archetypal combat general – 'the perfect fighting animal'. Rommel was a man who needed the catalyst of battle to transform the basically stolid elements of his Swabian temperament into the combination of ruthlessness and imaginative flair which took him, in four years of war and two years of actual fighting, from obscure Lieutenant Colonel to Field Marshal and a secure place in the history of German arms.

To the military historian, one of the most striking features of Rommel's career is its similarity to that of Montgomery, the British general whom he faced in North Africa in a remarkable campaign of personal confrontation. A study of the lives of these two men produces an extraordinary sensation of inevitability – an impression that from the very beginning they were both being directed, by forces outside their own control, along converging paths leading to their trial of strength in the Western Desert. Both were born and brought up outside the military caste of their countries; of both it can be said that they showed little or no interest in women until they married – and that they never looked at any other women afterwards (although in Montgomery's case the tragedy of his wife's sudden death was a crucial factor in his subsequent development). Both Montgomery and Rommel spent an important part of their lives between the wars evolving, formulating and eventually publishing the principles of infantry training and tactics which were to provide the basic doctrine upon which the armies of their respective countries went to war with each other in 1939; yet both eventually made their military reputation as practitioners of fluid armoured warfare. Both marked their first experience of active service with exploits of personal leadership and physical courage – in 1914 Montgomery led a bayonet charge on a trench full of Germans near the village of Meteren in Northern France; almost simultaneously and not very far away young Lieutenant Rommel was leading three of his men in a desperate assault on fifteen or twenty Frenchmen; both were wounded in action in the same year. Both received, as subalterns, decorations for bravery normally reserved for senior officers – Montgomery the DSO and Rommel the *Pour le Mérite*.

Between the wars Rommel's career (again the comparison

with Montgomery is irresistible) was unspectacular, but worthy, conscientious and efficient. It was only when the two men came face to face in the desert that the essential difference between them became dramatically evident. Whereas Montgomery was meticulous in his planning, painstaking in his preparations for battle, and cautious in his tactical approach, Rommel was imaginative, dashing and intuitive – often to the point of rashness. He was never able fully to accept the fact that for the German High Command his role in North Africa was largely a diversionary and subsidiary affair, and that the minds of his masters in Berlin were concentrated more upon the Russians than upon the British Eighth Army.

Charles Douglas-Home has drawn a vivid picture of Rommel's complex personality. From it emerges a man who wrote homely, affectionate letters to his wife in the heat of battle, but who was able, apparently, coldly to shoot dead a French officer who refused to obey his orders after being taken prisoner; a rather dull, unexciting man who only came to life when hunting gazelle from his staff car or careering about the battlefield in the armoured command vehicle which he had appropriated for his own use after its original owner, General O'Connor, had been captured by the Germans in 1941.

For a while Rommel became a superhuman figure in the hagiology of the British soldier – a figure so glamorous and omnipotent that the British High Command had to mount a special propaganda campaign designed to deflate his reputation. He died disgraced, blackmailed into suicide by the Nazis after the attempt on Hitler's life in 1944. Although Rommel denied to the end that he had been involved in the bomb plot, questions of guilt or innocence were marginal considerations in the Third Reich. It is in many ways a paradigm of the recurrent tragedy of war, a terrible, absorbing story of a great battlefield general, deploying his military talents unquestioningly in the service of an evil regime; and being murdered in the end, with the inevitability of a Greek tragedy, by the men who had used for their own ends, his undoubted qualities of patriotism, loyalty and leadership.

Lord Chalfont

1 Baptism of Fire

THE GERMANY into which young Erwin Rommel was born on 15 November 1891, was without doubt a country fit for a Field Marshal, but perhaps not for the kind of Field Marshal which Rommel was destined to become. He was born at Heidenheim, near Ulm, the capital of the state of Württemberg. Rommel's father was a schoolteacher, specialising in mathematics, as had his father before him. His mother was the daughter of a former president of the government of Württemberg. The Rommel family circle typified the stolid, worthy world of middle-class officialdom in provincial Germany, tinged with the practicality, commonsense and unemotionalism which is said to be the hallmark of all Swabians from that corner of south-west Germany.

Until the beginning of the nineteenth century, the area that eventually became Germany was a patchwork of small independent states, like Württemberg, which existed under the competing influences of Austria and Prussia. After 1830, these states started to join forces with Prussia, first in a customs union, the Zollverein, which was a free trade area under Prussian leadership, and then to advance step by step into a political union which culminated in the Second Reich – the German Empire – in 1871.

Naturally, the militaristic character of the Second Reich was not immediately established, even in Prussia or the northern regions. South of the River Main, the states had a more liberal reputation than those of the north. The bourgeoisie there had no great love either for strong central governments or for the military. The army had held a relatively low place in Swabian society before 1870. Military service was looked on much more as the prerogative of aristocrats or the lower classes. By the time Rommel was born, the fusion of these states into an empire had the momentum of twenty-three years. He did not grow up a typical young Prussian militarist at all, and to the end of his life, his Swabian virtues of fairness and lack of extremism seemed unshakeable. But the society around him during boyhood, youth, even early maturity was one which could hardly be ignored, and must to some extent have conditioned him and helped shape his attitudes.

By the 1890s, the old liberalism and scepticism towards the military which before 1870 had been prevalent all over Germany – Prussia included – was almost extinguished under a wave of patriotism and pride of arms which followed the Prussian victories over Austria in 1866 and France in 1870.

PREVIOUS PAGES German infantry on the Isonzo front.

OPPOSITE Kaiser Wilhelm II, pinnacle of Prussian military pride, with his royal English cousin, George V.

A First World War painting
of a German reconnoitring
unit using a 'liquid fire
machine', better known as
a flame thrower.

14

Kaiser Wilhelm II, instructing a group of his generals. Aloof from the civilian world, the officer class felt it owed its allegiance to the Kaiser alone.

Though the states remained semi-independent within the Reich, young Germans came to discover that the one common experience that they had was service in the army. The armies remained technically separate until 1918, but after 1871 their training and outlook was standardised – and they soon became completely dominated by the traditions and influence of the Prussian army.

The army then began to enjoy a much greater measure of social prestige. It was no longer a haven merely for aristocrats and peasants. The bourgeoisie flocked to join it. When they

failed to attain regular commissions, they joined the Reserve. Society as a whole became permeated with military attitudes too. A general obeisance to and reverence for the royal army took hold. Indeed, it extended to the wearer of any uniform. The rigidity of the military hierarchy infected the outside world, and carried these attitudes to seniority and status into civilian life and into the bureaucracy. The warm afterglow of Prussia's military victories was fanned with German nationalism, and the heat welded the empire still more firmly into one unit. The schools to which young Rommel went during the 1890s were teaching that it was the royal army which had gloriously achieved the new unity of Germany; the unification process was depicted entirely in terms of the victories, as though the army alone was the agent of this complicated historical process.

The anniversary of the formation of the Reich took second place to the anniversary of the battle of Sedan, which had confirmed Germany's victory over France in 1870. Society thrilled to the endless rhythm of military bands, the erection of martial monuments, the whole ordered pomp and self-importance of a people stuffed out with ceremonial. It is true that in the south, where Rommel grew up, this respect for the uniform, any uniform, was less marked than in the north. But gradually, as the old order changed under the press of industrialisation, expansion and prosperity, the army assumed a more respectable place even in south German society. The old idealism associated with Prussian puritanism, sacrifice and service was replaced with a new spirit of materialism and cynicism. Externally, the army seemed the only body determined to stand out against this decadence. Internally, this was not the case. Morality was condoned only if it was orthodox; independent minds were discouraged. The officer class was impressed with the fact that it owed its allegiance to the Kaiser alone. The Kaiser himself, addressing new recruits at this time, told them that they must be prepared to fire on their parents if need be, in the cause of the Reich. He described the Reichstag and its deputies as 'a rabble without a country'. Under these influences, how could the officer class avoid becoming more and more aloof from the civilian world, more and more subject only to the political control of the Kaiser? Later, when the Kaiser was deposed after 1918, the army was reconstituted and was called on to show allegiance to the Weimar Republic. It naturally did so with a certain amount of distaste.

17

Later still, during the rise of Hitler, it might have moved itself
to defend the values of Weimar if it had ever embraced them.
But nostalgia for the old order was still strong, and the army –
reared in this tradition of apolitical allegiance whatever the
social consequences – went down to Hitler almost without a
fight.

When Rommel died, at the age of fifty-two, he had served
in the German army for just over thirty-four years. Of those
thirty-four, just over six were spent in battlefield conditions.
His exploits during those years of battle were so spectacular
that it is easy to forget what a very large part of his adult life,
indeed of his whole life, was spent not on the battlefield, but in
an environment which must have been partly conditioned by
the peacetime military or the middle-class world of the time.
Out of battle, he was in a sense indistinguishable from the
thousands of other provincial middle-class Germans who
grew up in the bosom of the thrusting young Reich; who saw
it collapse at the end of their youth; who, as young men in
their thirties and forties, saw it rise again as a psychotic
phoenix under Hitler and finally disappear in the ashes of the
Berlin bunker as they approached middle age.

The most important parts of Rommel's life are, clearly
compressed into a few electrifying years of battlefield service
between 1914 and 1917 and again from 1940 to 1943. But to
understand the paradoxes of the man, one must see the kind of
background from which he came, and to which he used to go
home, which informed him as a man, and as a German – if not
as a general – and that background is essentially one of small-
town Germany. On the battlefield, Rommel was often a man
of genius; off it, he was essentially a small-town German with
a drabness about him that hardly seems compatible with the
romanticised image his military exploits have earned for him.

Of all the great names who belong to the history of German
arms between 1860 and 1940, Rommel stands out as a man
apart. The history of German arms and the German army
tends to be seen in terms of the general staff, which dominated
the organisation and development of the army at a time at
which individual commanders were becoming subordinate to
the idea of total war, and to the massive power and organisation which an industrial state could apply to the business of
war if it was properly mobilised. Naturally, individuals had a
great influence on these developments, from the Gneisenau
and Scharnhorst revolutions of 1806 through a line which

18

Rommel as a junior officer
with the Württemberg 124th
Infantry Regiment,
First World War.

OPPOSITE Frau Lucie Maria
Rommel (née Mollin), whom
Rommel married in Danzig,
when on leave from the front
in November 1916.

included the two von Moltkes, von Schlieffen, Ludendorff,
von Seeckt, Schleicher, Halder and even Guderian. But the
great significance of these men is that they made their contribution from the centre. Rommel made his from the wings. In
their writing and thinking and organising, they changed the
German army by developing its central organisation and
philosophy. Rommel did not belong to this great general staff
tradition. His effect on the German army and its tactics came
through the example he gave on the field of battle, rather than
through any administrative or policy-making process at the
level of grand strategy or in the general staff.

Rommel was an outsider as far as the general staff was concerned. It was not just that his social origins were not equal to
the 'vons' – the junker counts and the patrician families who
had traditionally provided so many cadres for the small self-
perpetuating body of officers who, with great skill, kept their
hold on the German general staff. It was that all his life he was
more at home in the execution of decisions than in the formu-
lation of policy. He was an instinctive rather than an intellectual fighter. In peacetime, Rommel showed none of the fire
and imagination of his battlefield exploits. It took the smell of
gunpowder, almost literally, to excite his senses.

Rommel was not, however, an outsider from the great
generality of the German army to which he belonged for so
long and within which his career at first developed along such
very conventional lines. His military career took him from a
teenager to a man well into his forties as a more or less straight-
forward, uncomplicated, reasonably compliant member of
that military community which grew up in the Second Reich
and which showed remarkable powers of survival through all
the buffetings which it received between 1910 and 1940.

Rommel joined the army in July 1910, having abandoned
his first thought of becoming an engineer. He signed up with
his local infantry regiment, the 124th (6th Württemberg),
starting as an officer cadet, which meant serving in the ranks
before being sent on to the war school. After three months, he
was promoted Corporal, after six Sergeant, and in March 1911
went to the officers' military school at Danzig. He was commissioned the following January and then returned to his
regiment in Weingarten.

While he was in Danzig, Rommel met and fell in love with
a young language student, Lucie Maria Mollin, the daughter
of a Prussian landowner and the cousin of a colleague in the

military academy. They did not become formally engaged until 1915, but were married in 1916, and then went through twelve years of marriage without a child. Manfred, their only child, was born in 1928. After he met Lucie – Lu as he came to call her – Rommel appears never to have looked at another woman – possibly he had not looked at one before, either. But after 1911, until his death, there was a constancy in his emotional and family life which is almost uncanny – he was slightly formal, fair but strict and astoundingly punctilious about writing letters to her, sometimes two or three on the same day, even when on the battlefield. His emotional upsets, such as they were, seemed to be entirely concerned with his military world. His wife and son provided a backcloth to his life which came to life and colour only at the very end, when he chose, under duress, to take his own life as much for their sake as for his own.

For the two years before the outbreak of war, Rommel was a young subaltern in charge of recruits at Weingarten. By all accounts, he was the epitome of a conscientious, efficient but rather dull young regimental officer, mature before his time, fair to his juniors, respected rather than loved, and that perhaps more for his proficiency than for his humanity. He showed every sign of turning into a good major at the end of a long, worthy but essentially unimaginative career in regimental soldiering.

All this was to change when Rommel went to war. He fought with great distinction through the First World War as a young infantry officer, winning medals for bravery which were normally reserved for senior officers. He was lucky to spend much less of his war in the trenches than did most other young men of his age, on either side. Indeed, most of his battle experience was gained in conditions in which he was given a much freer hand as a junior officer than he might have had in the trenches.

After the war, Rommel was to write about his exploits in a slim volume called *Infantry Attacks* which became a kind of training manual for the German infantry. It was illustrated with his own sketches, and showed early signs of the graphic narrative power which races through his diaries of the Second World War. In those later diaries, one gets the worm's-eye-view of war but enhanced with the perspective given by the commander. In *Infantry Attacks*, it is merely the worm's-eye-view of a junior officer in the infantry. But slim and modest

22

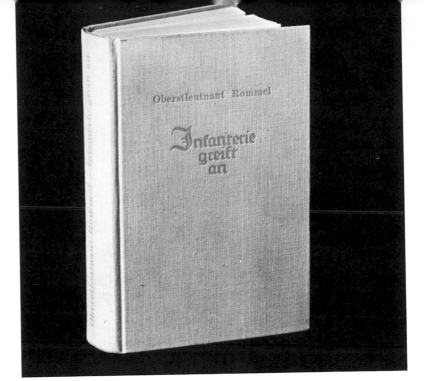

Rommel's manual *Infanterie greift an* (*Infantry Attacks*), based on his First World War fighting experience, is full of clear-sighted discussion of infantry tactics, and earned Rommel a considerable reputation.

One of the many diagrams in Rommel's *Infanterie greift an* which he sketched himself.

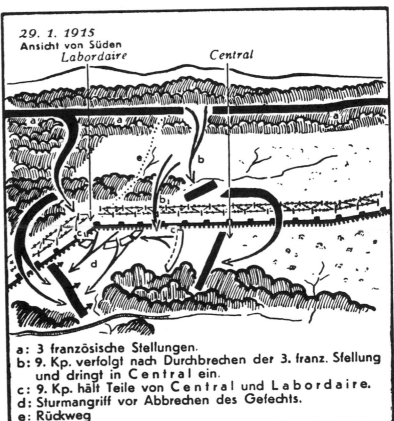

29. 1. 1915
Ansicht von Süden
Labordaire   Central

a: 3 französische Stellungen.
b: 9. Kp. verfolgt nach Durchbrechen der 3. franz. Stellung und dringt in C e n t r a l ein.
c: 9. Kp. hält Teile von C e n t r a l und L a b o r d a i r e.
d: Sturmangriff vor Abbrechen des Gefechts.
e: Rückweg

23

though the volume was, it had a revolutionary effect on
Rommel's subsequent career. It was brought to Hitler's attention during the 1930s, and Rommel with it. The result was
that, whereas he might have spent the Second World War as
an infantry officer, perhaps commanding an infantry division
or an army corps, and probably perishing in Russia or
Normandy because of his passion for the front line, instead he
became a Field Marshal.

On 2 August 1914, Rommel's regiment marched out to war,
with bands playing, drums beating, crowds cheering. They
were on their way to the 'threatened frontier' in the west. But
Rommel was not with them. He had to stay behind in Weingarten for a few days to bring up reserves, champing lest he
miss the first fight. He need not have worried. A few days
later, he was at the front of the battlelines, savouring his first
taste of a way of life which changed him from the shy, conscientious young man that he was, into what Brigadier Desmond
Young, in his biography, *Rommel*, describes as 'the perfect
fighting animal'.

Rommel's first action was with three other men from his
platoon against fifteen or twenty Frenchmen whom he found
barring their way. Characteristically, he rushed at them,
shouting. He was repulsed, but this instant reaction to finding
himself in a tight corner was one which he was going to
demonstrate over and over again in his combat career. In his
second action, a few days later, Rommel collapsed from sheer
exhaustion and the severe stomach trouble which was to
plague him throughout his life. He was reprimanded for being
found asleep, and for falling off his horse from sheer fatigue.
Late in September 1914, he was wounded in the leg when,
typically, he charged three Frenchmen with a bayonet because
he had run out of ammunition. Back in the line, in the Argonne
area, in January 1915, he won his first decoration for bravery.
Another nine months in the trenches followed before Rommel
was posted to a mountain unit, in which his talents as an
infantry subaltern with plenty of dash, initiative and energy
could be put to better use than in the static trench warfare on
Germany's Western Front. He spent a quiet spring and
summer in mountain training in the ridge of South Hilsen,
and was then posted to the Eastern Front at Siebenbürgen to
take part in operations against the Rumanians.

By a historical irony, it was as a company commander
against the Rumanians that Rommel found himself in a situa-

25

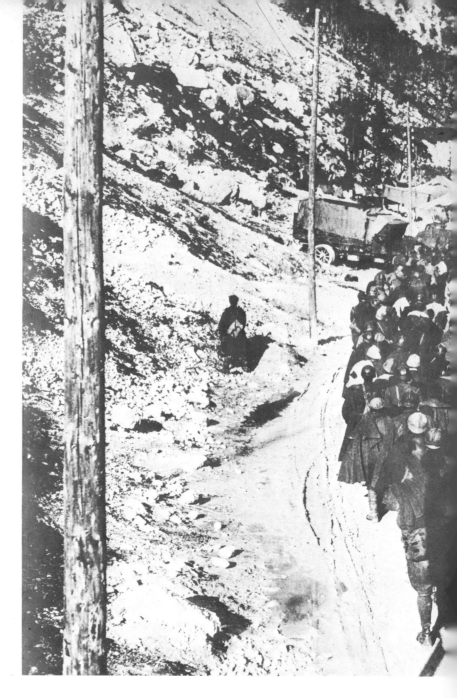

Italians captured in the Isonzo valley: Rommel crowned his First World War career here by winning the *Pour le Mérite* for an action during which some 9,000 Italian troops were taken prisoner.

tion which was to be reversed to his disadvantage many years later when he was commanding the German army in Africa. During one company advance, he gave orders to a platoon commander not to advance farther. The junior officer, seeing what he thought was an exploitable opening, disobeyed and advanced deeper into the enemy lines. Then he called for help to consolidate his position, which was otherwise too much

26

exposed. Rommel was angry, and said that no help could
come. 'I was none too elated with this course of events. Why
did the platoon fail to stay in its place as ordered? Should I
commit my last reserves as requested by the platoon commander? No, little as I liked it, I could not help the platoon.'
Years later, the same situation overtook him, but in reverse.
He, too, in command of the African forces, was instructed not

to advance. Yet advance he did, and in a most spectacular and convincing way. But when he called Berlin for help to hold his new and much extended position, no help came. By the tone of his great disappointment at the time, it is doubtful if he remembered the early strategic lesson which he himself had taught another junior officer in the Carpathians.

In May 1917, Rommel found himself back on Hilsen ridge facing the French. Then, in August, he returned to the Carpathian front, where his actions against the Rumanians and Italians were to climax his First World War career, first in August, in the assault on the heavily-fortified Rumanian position at Mount Cosna, and in October, against the Italians at Caporetto. At the end of the battle of Caporetto, writes Brigadier Young, 'He had been continuously on the move for

A military encampment on Red Tower Pass in the Rumanian mountains. Much of the fighting between the Rumanian/Italian and the Austrian/German forces took place in extremely difficult conditions.

fifty hours, had covered 12 miles as the crow flies in mountainous country, had climbed up to 7000 feet and had captured 150 officers, 9000 men and 81 guns' – all this, ironically, after he had had orders not to attack! For his action at Caporetto, Rommel was awarded the '*Pour le Mérite*' which was normally won only by generals and had been awarded to only about two or three junior officers before him. He was also promoted Captain. But his war was now effectively over. One or two further exploits followed Caporetto but, too soon for his own tastes, he was posted away to a junior staff appointment, in which he stayed until the end of the war.

So these brief but spectacular campaigns as a young man were all the fighting experience Rommel was to gain until nearly twenty-three years later, when, approaching middle age, he led a tank division across France. His innate characteristics remained consistent as he passed on up an ever-ascending scale of military power, with the attendant inhibitions and complications of effective command. Yet these early experiences of war must also have left their mark on him, for he always seemed to think of battle as a kind of wild dance, an adventure, in which he had to pit his imagination – actually his genius – against improbable odds. The tactical acrobatics which he performed as an infantry subaltern naturally became much more difficult with larger formations. Perhaps they were also less compatible with the role of an army commander in the huge and complex effort required of a nation at war and fighting on several fronts.

However, even in 1917, Rommel's tactical techniques showed themselves to be the natural and inspired precursors of the Blitzkrieg principles which were later codified by Captain B.H. Liddell Hart in England and adopted by the Germans during the mid-1930s. They were then put into devastating effect in the opening campaigns of the Second World War. Rommel's tactics relied basically on deep penetration behind enemy lines, and unhesitating decisions to attack in the rear. He always assumed that the rear areas would capitulate to a surprise offensive. When he assaulted a position, he immediately set about securing the flanks of his narrow bridgehead and then pushing as many forces as possible on through the gap which he had created and secured, so that they broke out and expanded on the other side – tactics which, years later, Liddell Hart was to describe as the 'expanding torrent'.

29

2 Between the Wars

SIX WEEKS AFTER THE ARMISTICE of November 1918, Captain Rommel was reposted to his old regiment at Weingarten, and prepared to settle down in the same barracks in which he had enlisted as a young officer cadet eight years previously. In the summer of 1919, he was sent to Friedrichshafen to command an internal security company. In January 1921, he was promoted to the command of an infantry regiment at Stuttgart, remaining there as a captain for nine years. There seemed but few highlights. In 1927, he and Lu went on leave to Italy to revisit the scenes of his former triumphs. Armed with a camera he took the first of many thousands of pictures which he later used to illustrate his war diaries. In 1928, on Christmas Eve, his son Manfred was born. In October of the next year, Rommel was posted as an instructor to the infantry school at Dresden. It was while lecturing there on his Great War experiences that he had the idea of publishing his lectures as the manual, *Infantry Attacks*. In October 1933, he was promoted Major and sent to Goslar to command a mountain batallion, with which he stayed until October 1935, when he was sent as a lieutenant-colonel to teach at the war academy at Potsdam, just outside Berlin. In November 1938, he was appointed to command the war academy at Wiener Neustadt, leaving only shortly before the outbreak of war.

But, by then, the years of obscurity were already over for him. A month earlier, when Hitler had marched into the Sudetenland, Rommel had been in attendance as the commander of his bodyguard. He had at last come to the Führer's attention. Six years from that first assignment for the dictator, Hitler was to give orders that Rommel was to die. But during those years he was to catapult the brilliant officer into high rank, give him an army, an independent command (a rare, almost unique phenomenon under Hitler) and finally promote him to the rank of Field Marshal. How had those placid and domestic years of peacetime soldiering prepared Rommel for such an outsize but tragic destiny?

Between 1919 and 1938, Rommel's military career was modest, orthodox, almost tranquil, compared with the turbulence which raged about in German politics outside his family and regimental circle. Rommel seemed to arrive at that moment in 1939 at which war was declared almost as an innocent, largely untouched by the great convulsions of the 1920s and 1930s. In a sense, that is the reason for which he had been selected in the immediate aftermath of the first war, but to

PREVIOUS PAGES President Oskar von Hindenburg, surviving representative of Germany's former imperial glory, greets the new Chancellor, Adolf Hitler.

32

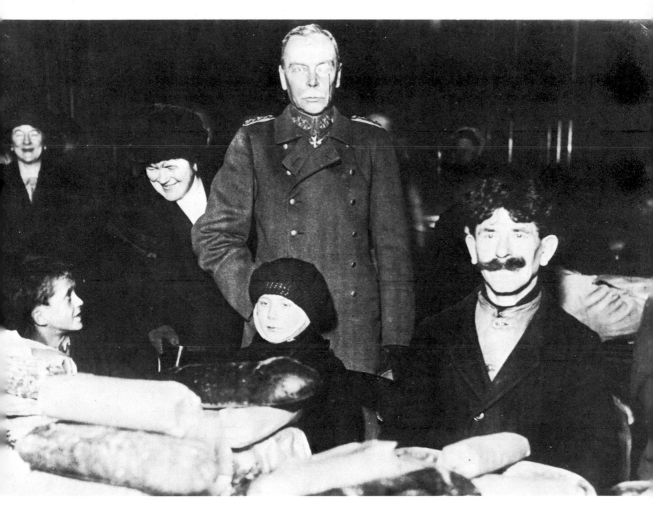

General von Seeckt visiting a Christmas charity dinner organised for needy families in 1923.

understand the full extent of Rommel's insulation from these events, it is necessary to go back to November 1918, when the Kaiser was deposed and Germany surrendered to the Allies.

The country's collapse was total. There was disintegration at home and defeat in the field. It is true that the myth of the 'stab in the back' – that the German army was let down by Berlin politicians when it was still quite capable of defending the country – gained some currency in the years immediately following the war, and particularly following what were seen as the humiliating terms of the Versailles Peace Treaty. But compared with the subsequent dismemberment of Germany in 1945, the 1918 peace formula was a respectable affair.

At the time of the armistice, Germany was ruled by a council of deputies and by the general staff. Both the political and

The shortage of food, resulting from the post-war collapse, led to scenes such as this one in a Munich street, where a horse is being eagerly dismembered.

military leadership feared the rise of Bolshevik groups in the country, and the prospect that Germany would be torn in two by civil war between Bolshevik groups and the right-wing bands which were also forming. Even the army itself was in danger of internal disintegration into soldiers' councils and local groups of young officers and NCOs who objected to the armistice and were later to form what became known as the Free Corps. Rommel had some personal experience of this when he had to cross Germany soon after the war to bring Lu home to Weingarten from Danzig and was jostled and insulted by hostile groups of citizens on the way. The period which he spent in charge of the internal security company at Friedrichshafen was characterised also by a certain taste for lawlessness shown in both the unit he was commanding and the society

34

GARMISCH~PARTENKIRCHENER
VOLKSWEHR bringtgefangene

Politics at street level: revolutionary 'red guards' in Garnisch-Partenkirchen in Bavaria have been arrested by the local *Volkswehr* (People's Army), c. 1921.

outside. But he himself showed no inclination to get involved even in military politics.

The army's Chief-of-Staff at the time was General von Seeckt, who masterminded the transition from the large royal army of the now vanished Reich, into the select cadre which soldiered on during Germany's twilight years of the 1920s, until it was ready to provide the basis for Hitler's great military expansion in the 1930s. Von Seeckt had to nurse the army through a period of great loss: the loss of its figurehead – the Kaiser – and the loss of that image of the German Reich which had sustained it and had been the absolute focus of its energies for fifty years. He had to see that something replaced the monarchy as the object of the army's loyalty and as a source of their ultimate purpose and inspiration.

35

In the end, this became nothing more than a spirit of self-preservation. The survival of the German army as an independent organism during the 1920s nourished von Seeckt and his officers more than any other ulterior purpose. A vague, rather nebulous idea of the need to preserve some expression of cohesion within the German commonwealth may have provided a slightly larger context of inspiration. But basically, von Seeckt's legacy to the German army was to inculcate an effective will and instinct for survival, yet at the price of ignoring those other forces which were at work among the remaining German population – a population clearly less single-minded, less dedicated, less preoccupied with this one predominant purpose than were von Seeckt's chosen men.

For the Peace Conference at Versailles, von Seeckt proposed that Germany should retain a unified army of 400,000 men, but that the army's traditional judicial and political autonomy within Germany should be abolished so that it could no longer be regarded as a state within the state. This figure was initially reduced to 300,000, and by the end of the Peace Conference, von Seeckt had had to accept an army reduced to a strength of 100,000 men, of whom only 4,000 would be officers. The German army was aghast at the peace terms. In March 1920, there was an attempt by the Free Corps to stage a right-wing *putsch* against the government and the general staff. A detachment of the Free Corps marched on Berlin. The government retreated to Dresden, and then to Stuttgart. In four days, the *putsch* crumbled, but in the meantime von Seeckt had found himself forced more and more to perform

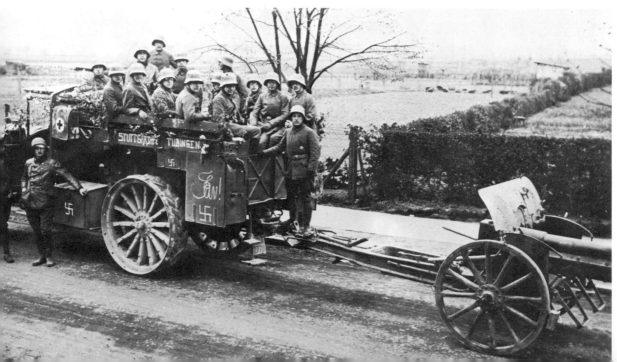

ABOVE General von Seeckt
inspecting the troops of his
small but ambitious post-war
army in an autumn
manœuvre, 1926.

LEFT Troops of Rommel's
own Württemberg regiment
were used for peace keeping
duties in the explosive
situation of post-war
Munich.

the function of the traditional Commander-in-Chief, a post
which had been abolished under the peace terms.

He was acutely conscious of the danger of a war breaking out
within the army itself, and strove to prevent this by insisting
that officers should insulate themselves from politics. In this,
Rommel was, for von Seeckt, the archetype of the young
officer whom he planned to retain in the four thousand
allowed him. Von Seeckt's mission after Versailles was not
only to preserve the German army at the size laid down by the
victorious powers at the Conference, but to organise it entirely
as a cadre for expansion some day into a much larger army. He
used to say that he did not know when Germany would again
need a large army; he knew only that she would. His young
officers were thus picked with great care from the pool left

The right-wing *Freikorps* 'Werdenfels' stages a quasi-military march on Munich.

over from the imperial army, which had never been entirely disembodied after the armistice. They all knew that their historic mission was to husband Germany's military resources for a better day. At the time, it was only natural for a young German like Rommel – of patriotic inclination and no great political sensitivity – to accept all von Seeckt's premises and work for the day on which the German army could once more come into its own.

In all this, Rommel was no exception to the generality of all those other young officers who made up von Seeckt's four thousand. Of course, the army was not entirely immune from the political alarums which broke out periodically in Germany during that time. Hitler had infected young officers here and there, and when he proclaimed his first abortive *coup* in

Munich in 1923, a number of them rallied to him, particularly from the Infantry School. They were later dismissed.

Von Seeckt retired in 1926 and was succeeded by General Schleicher, who had to contend with the rise of Hitler's private party army, the SA or Stormtroopers, but who never fully recognised the danger which this organisation presented. He was intrigued by its potential, since it consisted mostly of former officers and men who had not been able to stay in uniform when the army was cut to peacetime proportions. He clearly hoped that, by co-operating with them, the army might be able gradually to bring them under its control, and to this effect some arrangements were made whereby army training depots gave military instruction to SA groups. But the army itself never seemed to be wholly convinced. In Ulm, close to Rommel's home, two subalterns in an artillery regiment were found to have formed Nazi cells and were dismissed. When Hitler assumed power in 1933, Schleicher, who had briefly preceded him as Chancellor, made noises suggesting that the army would resist the Nazi regime. But they were only noises, and there was no resistance.

With Hitler as Chancellor, the SA started to flex its muscles. It now numbered about 400,000 in twenty-four army groups, clearly reminiscent of the old Free Corps. It continually asked the army for instructors. The army kept a watchful eye on it, but friction increased. As the SA leader Röhm became more and more importunate, the two armies – SA and regular – seemed bound for total duplication of their training and command functions. Then, on 30 June 1934, in 'the night of the long knives', Röhm was arrested and killed, along with many other of Hitler's opponents. A month later, President Hindenburg died and Hitler achieved supreme power as both President and Chancellor. For the army, it was a crucial moment at which they were required to sign a new oath of allegiance to the Führer and Chancellor in one.

The oath of allegiance was one more momentary worry for the army, coming on top of the growing internal unease which the rise of the private organisations had provoked between those officers whose political sympathies lay with the Nazis and those whose traditional view was that the Stormtroopers were bad for the regular army and therefore bad for Germany. Rommel obviously must have been aware of the strains within the army, but this does not seem to have affected him unduly. His first brush with the new order was modest, arising out of

'Germany awake' reads the
Nazi Party banner at
Nuremberg in 1927. With
Hitler are (left to right)
Himmler, Hess, unknown,
Strasser and SA leader
Wildenbruch.

R.P. Nürnberg 1927.

his pride in his unit rather than from any deep-seated ideological antipathy to the Nazi party, and it did not occur until 1935. Rommel's mountain battalion at Goslar had been chosen to provide a guard of honour for the Führer himself. Rommel was told shortly before the parade that a single file of ss men would take position in front of his troops, to look after Hitler's safety. He told the ss that his battalion would not turn out under these conditions. He was asked to see Himmler and Goebbels, to whom he then explained that he thought that the proposal was an insult to his battalion. They agreed, and the proposal was dropped. The parade took place without the ss file, and Hitler's safety was adequately looked after by Rommel's mountaineers. At this meeting, Rommel met Hitler only officially as the guard of honour commander, and it was not until later, when he had been commander of Hitler's permanent bodyguard in the drive into Sudetenland, that he started to get on reasonably close terms with the Führer.

Considering his proximity to Hitler after coming to the Führer's attention, Rommel kept remarkably clear of any party or political involvement. It was naturally in keeping with Rommel's character and outlook to regard the private armies, the sa and ss, with considerable distaste – perhaps as a temporary aberration with which the Führer would soon dispense when his power was consolidated. But it would also have been in keeping with his character only to observe and not to involve himself with the moral, political or philosophical implications of something of which he knew so little. Things which were happening in Germany, even within the army itself, and which were outside his immediate focus seemed remote to a man like Rommel, with his innate practicality and remarkable narrowness of interest and perspective.

Was he, for instance, affected by the new oath? It is not known. Was he any more alarmed than most other German citizens by the Röhm massacre? Doubtless not. Did he register concern at the subsequent intrigue and blackmail used by Hitler to discredit his War Minister and Commander-in-Chief? There is no sign.

Of the Führer himself, Rommel clearly shared the view of most Germans, though, as war became more imminent, not the view of the general staff. After 1935, the army was embarked on a colossal programme of expansion which in a sense fulfilled all the careful and clandestine preparations which had been laid originally by von Seeckt. But it did more than that.

'Rommel kept remarkably clear of any party or political involvement'

OPPOSITE Party Day, Nuremberg 1938: Germany was on the march as never before.

42

The purity and absolute dedication of the von Seeckt army obviously suffered in the heady expansion. New men came in, and the preoccupations of expansion took many senior officers' minds off the unwelcome effects of Nazi rule which were evident to those who wanted to look. Between 1932 and 1938, the number of generals rose from thirty-two to nearly four hundred. But Rommel was not among them.

In June 1937, Hitler ordered his forces to keep themselves in a permanent state of readiness for immediate mobilisation. Of course, they were not technically, nor indeed psychologically, ready for any kind of war. In February 1938, Hitler removed his War Minister and army Commander-in-Chief after the most amazing sage of blackmail, intrigue and skulduggery which involved some unsavoury exposures of the methods used by the regime against those whom it disliked. Later that year, in August, General Beck, the Chief-of-Staff, resigned when he saw that his attempts to induce the general staff to prevent the inevitable slide towards war had failed. A month later, his successor, General Halder, organised a plot to unseat Hitler, but was foiled by Chamberlain's decision to visit Munich and conclude the ill-fated agreement with the Führer. The amazing thing about Germany's onrush to war after 1938 is how little the general staff seemed to want war and how powerless they apparently were to prevent its happening. There was widespread plotting and dissatisfaction with Hitler, which continued right into the war. There is no sign, however, that Rommel was ever privy to these early movements of dissidence, probably because at that period he was still comparatively junior and certainly right outside the small circle of general staff officers who still held the real positions of influence within the army, even if the army as a whole had such little influence outside.

For all that, when war was declared, Rommel – recently promoted Major-General – was once again at Hitler's side. Throughout the Polish campaign, he commanded the Führer's bodyguard and was obviously well placed at the centre to see the devastating effect achieved by the invading German Panzer divisions applying all the tactical principles of the Blitzkrieg. When the campaign was finished, Hitler asked him what command he would like. In his own words, Rommel made the 'immoderate' request for a Panzer division, 'though many others were more qualified' and though, as he later confided, it did 'not suit the gentlemen at the Army

44

The Poland campaign brought Rommel his first experience of Hitler as a military commander. Elevation to the Führer's staff and the lightning success of Germany's attack were both exhilarating experiences after so many years out of active service.

Headquarters'. The request was granted. On 15 February 1940, Rommel assumed command of the 7th Panzer Division. His predecessor in command of the division was General Stumme. Though he did not know it at the time, it was hardly a good omen. When Rommel returned to fight and lose the second battle of Alamein, thirty-four months later, it was again General Stumme whom he came to replace. But in the meantime, there was a harvest of triumphs to be won, and, more important, Rommel, the fighting animal, was back in the fight. The years of mediocrity were behind him for good.

3 Race Across France

ON 10 MAY 1940, the day on which Churchill became Prime Minister of Great Britain, Hitler invaded the West. In the space of a week, his Panzer divisions had burst through Holland and Belgium to reach the Channel coast. Within three weeks, the remnants of the British Expeditionary Force – a quarter of a million men – had been evacuated across the Channel in any vessel they could find. On 5 June, the Germans were on the Somme; on the 9th they crossed the Seine; on the 14th they entered Paris; they had reached the Rhône valley by the 16th. That same night, a new French Cabinet under Marshal Pétain sent Hitler a request for an armistice, which was in effect a notice of capitulation. There was some token negotiation while the Nazi divisions roared on. When France's surrender became effective on 25 June, it was a bare six weeks since the German tanks had first rolled forward into the hilly and wooded country of the Ardennes.

The German army's success had been spectacular, though neither inevitable nor predictable. When the offensive was launched, the Germans had 136 divisions against an equivalent of 156 divisions in the allied British, French, Dutch and Belgian armies. The Germans had 2,800 tanks, against 4,000 for the Allies, and their tanks were in no technical way superior to those of the Allies. Only in the air were the Germans superior in both the numbers and the quality of their fighter-bombers, but this need not have been – indeed was not – a decisive superiority.

The Germans' decisive advantage lay not so much in their technical superiority as in the way in which they used their divisions, particularly in the tactics of deep and narrow penetration which had been pioneered throughout the 1930s by a small group of German Panzer officers led by Heinz Guderian. In May 1940, he was commanding a Panzer corps which was to form the spearhead of the German offensive and advance so fast that it frightened Hitler almost as much as it frightened the French. In fact, only ten of the German divisions were armoured, but most of them were used with devastating effect by concentrating them on a narrow front. Yet there was nothing inevitable about their victory. Allied blunders throughout the lightning campaign gave a quite unjustified aura of invincibility to the Panzers. It might have been a very different story had the British and French previously made any attempt to study the implications of this kind of Blitzkrieg attack. There were great potential weaknesses in the technique, pro-

PREVIOUS PAGES German soldiers advancing through France pass a scattered heap of French steel helmets, mute witnesses to the abandoned defence of the town.

48

vided the defending forces maintained their balance and kept their nerve. But in 1940, the Allies did neither of these things.

As it was, the whole campaign for the fall of France, Belgium and Holland was split into two distinct phases. The first three weeks until 5 June consisted of two advances by the German forces. The northern advance, across a fairly broad front into Holland and northern Belgium, managed to lure forward the Allied divisions to meet what they expected to be the main German attack along the Channel coast. The other, and as it turned out more menacing attack involved three Panzer corps on the German léft flank, advancing initially through the Ardennes forest region, which all strategists had believed was impassable to armoured troops. From there, they swept round through Luxembourg and southern Belgium in a wide left-flanking movement which threatened to encircle the forward-placed Anglo-French divisions, to cut off their line of supplies from northern France, and perhaps even cut off the British from access to the Channel ports. By 5 June, they had routed the British and French armies, caused the complete evacuation of the British Expeditionary Force and overrun Belgium and Holland. They lay along the line of the River Somme, from the

General Heinz Guderian, outstanding personality in the development of tank warfare and *Blitzkrieg* techniques.

OPPOSITE General Franz Halder, Chief of Army General Staff who was an archetypal German staff officer and plotter *par excellence* – the epitome of all that Rommel was not.

'He led the division most of the time from the very front'

coastal area round Abbeville to the northern end of the old Maginot line of defences, which ran down the Franco-German border from Luxembourg to the Swiss frontier.

The second phase was from 5 to 25 June. The German forces executed three violent penetrations deep into the rest of France. On the right wing, on which Rommel and his division were, the forces went from Abbeville to Cherbourg and then on through Brittany and down the French west coast as far as Bordeaux. In the middle, the Panzers thrust straight into the heart of France, reaching Angoulême and Clermont Ferrand in the Massif Central by 25 June. On the left wing, Guderian's Panzer corps started by advancing due south to the Swiss frontier and then swung back eastwards towards the rear of the Maginot line to capture large numbers of French troops whom they surrounded and trapped against the Rhine.

Major-General Rommel's 7th Panzer Division was in the 15th Panzer Corps commanded by General Hoth. Like most of the other armoured divisions, Rommel's force made some quite spectacular advances during those summer days and nights. Perhaps its most decisive contribution to the overall campaign against France was in the crossing of the River Meuse, which took place after only two days of fighting. The glory and panache of that night-and-day runaway dash through a bewildered France was something common to most of the Panzers. But only Rommel's division was lucky to have at its head a man who not only led the division most of the time from the very front, who not only laid some of the guns himself, shouted orders to the infantry men going into assault, jumped on the turrets of leading tanks to replace wounded crewmen; who not only did these things in a manner quite uncharacteristic of the average divisional commander, but who also wrote it all down in a war diary of quite exceptional vividness and pace.

The contrast between the war diaries of Rommel and those of General Franz Halder, the army's Chief-of-Staff, tells almost all that needs telling about the difference between Rommel's kind of officer – the fighting, rather than thinking soldier – and that archetypal German staff officer who had been at the top of the general staff for the previous one hundred years. And what a contrast! In Berlin, the fastidious Halder, staff officer and plotter *par excellence*, is almost sensually methodical in his staff appreciations and planning notes; meticulously recording the administrative minutiae which are

50

Rommel and his staff hold
a hurried briefing in the
field. For the elated General
there were moments when
the war seemed more
like a picnic.

the lymph glands of military history; showing a twitch of pain
here and there at the Führer's excesses, or at some logistical
carelessness; but otherwise without emotion. Rommel, by
contrast, is in a paroxysm of movement and excitement as the
battle swirls round him; the narrative racing ahead with him
in the leading vehicle; a man possessed, sustained almost to
addiction by the adrenalin of war. There is no time for introspection, little for logistics, hardly a moment in which to
consider the foibles or faults of other people – friend or foe. In
a pause for breath, he writes an almost breathless note to the

faithful Lu: 'slept like a top, everything going well, don't worry,' or some such ritual exhortation. Before the battle, Halder is finding time to fuss about the late hours kept by young officers; in what currency should the soldiers receive their pay?; Hitler's nerves; has there been a leak? With Rommel: 'Dearest Lu, we're packing up at last; let's hope not in vain; don't worry yourself, everything will go all right.' Two days later, the day of the Meuse crossing, he came up for breath for the first time: 'everything is wonderful; I am hoarse from giving orders and shouting.'

A setback suffered by a German Panzer in a French coastal town. The headlong German advance was pursued with a calculated recklessness which was strongly opposed by many of the German General Staff and, indeed, by Hitler himself.

Rommel's natural courtesy and sense of marital duty would hardly have allowed him to admit to himself, let alone to Lu, that here, on the battlefield, he was closer to ecstasy than he could ever have been sitting by the hearth at Wiener Neustadt, however much he was to claim, some years later in the desert, that those years at the war academy were his happiest.

When Rommel had taken over his command in February, he had had no previous experience of Panzer warfare apart from what he had seen from his central position in Hitler's bodyguard during the Blitzkrieg into Poland the previous September. In the intervening period, he had tried to make up for this by intensive training with his division. But two months was hardly long enough, and though married to all those battlefield instincts which he had shown twenty-five years previously as a young infantry subaltern, Rommel's first few weeks in action were marked by administrative and command mix-ups which were clearly the products of over-enthusiasm and inexperience.

The pace and distance of the 7th Panzer Division's sweep from the German frontier to Cherbourg earned it the subsequent title of the 'Ghost Division'. A look at the map shows what a staggering advance it was for one division's work over six weeks, even by modern war standards. In his very first action, on 10 May, Rommel's division brushed through some fairly light opposition from French forces. Rommel, in character, had trained his men to react instantly and aggressively to any encounter. 'I've found again and again in encounter actions that the day goes to the side first to plaster the opponent with fire', he wrote. His motor-cyclists were trained to drive on with machine-guns firing at anything which smacked of the enemy. The whole division thus echoed the behaviour of that aggressive young man who had won his spurs in the Argonne.

By 12 May, Rommel's division had reached the River Meuse, where it found that the bridges at Dinant and Haux had just been blown by the retreating French. This was to be the division's first real test, and Rommel's. Indeed, the Meuse crossing was also the first real test of the whole invasion, and many would argue that its speedy outcome dictated the course of the rest of the campaign, at least psychologically, in the effect which it had on the morale of the French generals as much as on that of their men.

Certainly, the crossing involved Rommel's division in its first really hotly-contested action, of which there were not to be all that many more during its swift advance across northern France. To start with, the men recoiled from the fire which was bearing down on them from the French defenders on the other bank. Rommel was everywhere: giving orders along the bank; riding in the turret of a leading tank which was fired on several times; directing rifle companies himself; rallying his men and generally bringing the authority of his rank as divisional commander to bear decisively at the platoon and company level. Without doubt, it must have had a galvanising effect on the energies of his men, who must have been as unused as most private soldiers to the spectacle of their Major-General, a shadowy figure at the best of times, enduring the same dangers as themselves, and for all the world behaving like a junior officer and an apparently fearless one at that. Indeed, whatever rank he achieved, and whatever age,

The speed of the advance meant that German troops were strung out in a very thin, and had the Allies but known it, highly vulnerable line.

56

Rommel, with his youthful lust for battle, remained very much a junior officer at heart.

Rommel's 7th Panzer Division was not the only German division to cross the Meuse that day. But it was the one which most effectively consolidated its position on the far bank, and in that sense its crossing was perhaps the most decisive. Troops of Reinhardt's and Guderian's corps were also across, but were less solid on the western bank, and it was almost certainly the effect of Rommel's bridgehead which persuaded the French commander to order a general withdrawal to a new defensive line. In the ensuing confusion, the French opened up a gap in their line through which poured Guderian's Panzers until they had blasted a breach about sixty miles wide.

The breakout after the Meuse crossing soon brought the Panzers to the Channel coast. But the very speed and success of the sweep was very nearly its undoing. Hitler lost his nerve, and called a halt. He was haunted by the danger of the French army counter-attacking against the Germans on their by then very exposed and extended left flank. The commanders in the front line could see the improbability of this, in view of the total disorganisation which their sweeping attacks had caused in the French divisions. But back in Berlin there was less confidence. At Rommel's level, there was no sign or justification for Hitler's doubts, nor, indeed, was he affected by them. At Guderian's level, commanding the next corps, there was every sign.

'Their sweeping attacks caused total disorganisation in the French divisions'

On 15 May, General von Kleist, Guderian's superior commander, became nervous of the speed of the advance and ordered a twenty-four-hour halt. Guderian protested and secured a day's postponement for the order. But when it was finally enforced, on 17 May, he resigned his command, and was brought back the next day only after a compromise formula had been worked out with von Kleist, whereby he was allowed to continue advancing as a 'reconnaissance in force'. The whole front then started to advance again at speeds and over distances which were something previously unheard of in war. Reinhardt's corps achieved thirty-seven miles one day; Rommel's division fifty miles in one twenty-four-hour period, which included an unprecedented night march.

After the Meuse crossing on 13 May, and until he was brought to a temporary halt outside Arras by two British tank regiments, Rommel's advance was almost literally headlong. We see him in his armoured car, holding a conference with his

'Rommel was lucky
. . . many times
escaping while those
around him were
wounded or killed'

regimental commanders as they race along at forty mph, a whole column of vehicles behind him struggling to keep up. We see him negotiating for the speedier surrender of the garrison of Philippeville by giving permission for the French officers to keep their batmen and have their kit picked up for them. But the scene is not always so light-hearted. In one incident in the crush of vehicles, Rommel came across a staff car containing a French Lieutenant-Colonel. As Rommel and his column drove up, the Frenchman's 'eyes glowed hate and impotent fury and he gave the impression of being a thoroughly fanatical type'. They decided to take him on with them in one of their tanks, but the Colonel 'curtly refused three times to get into one of the tanks. There was nothing for it but to shoot him.'

Rommel was also very lucky. Time and again during the campaign, he exposed either himself individually or his whole division to risks which could have been disastrous had they been faced with a more collected enemy. Many times, Rommel escaped while those around him were wounded or killed.

As the Panzers crashed on through the night, we get a picture of French villagers rudely awakened by the din of vehicles and the shouting of soldiers; troops bivouacked by the road, 'their faces distorted with terror', lying huddled in ditches and hollows; refugee columns all over the roads, carts abandoned as their owners in panic fled into the fields. 'On we went at a steady speed, towards our objective', was the Panzer commander's laconic commentary.

Rommel's major advance in those first few days, towards the village of Le Câteau, was made with him leading the first column, believing that the rest of the division was following along rapidly behind. In this he was wrong: he was in fact alone with a Panzer battalion and part of a motor-cycle battalion. His division was strung out for miles behind him along a thin salient which was threatened on every side by French forces. As a result of his night march, he had far outstripped the other Panzer divisions on either flank. He set out in his armoured car to return along the line of his advance and look for the rest of the division. The French were still very much in evidence on either flank of the line of advance. Indeed, here and there they were still dominating the road itself. Rommel had to spend the whole day driving up and down the line looking for his scattered division and attempting to collect his

59

Rommel's impulsive style of command often carried him out of reach of his supporting troops, necessitating hasty consultation and reorientation.

troops. At any time, had the French been less demoralised and disorganised, a concerted attack on Rommel's undefended flanks would have been very serious for the Panzers. Rommel got away with it, though there were complaints from his staff at the breakdown of contact between them and their commander.

This was a complaint which was to be levelled again and again at Rommel – not without justification. His natural enthusiasm for the battle, and his profound belief that the commander must lead from the front, not only to infect his men with his confidence and enthusiasm but also to see for himself what was going on, naturally became more hazardous as the formations under his command became larger, and the

area covered by the battle more extensive. At the head of a Panzer division in France, it was easier for him to command in this way. He was part of a much larger front which was advancing at speed, and the quality of the opposition was clearly not presenting much of a threat. Indeed, one of the main impressions of Rommel's diary is how very few troops of the total divisional establishment of 12,500 he seemed to have with him most of the time. Because he was always at the front, or darting about looking for other units, there is none of the feeling of mass movement which one finds in other commanders' accounts of war, written from the centre.

At Arras, Rommel had, for a few moments at least, one of his most severe encounters in the French campaign. It was also the first time that he found himself fighting against British troops. His plans to by-pass Arras to the south, and swing round it, nearly foundered under the counter-attack by two British tank regiments. They represented the spear-head of two British divisions which had been ordered to counter-attack against the Germans, to protect the right flank of the British Expeditionary Force as it withdrew from Belgium back towards the Channel.

Rommel's encounter at Arras, though inevitably dramatic, was in fact only a very minor engagement. Yet this minor setback seemed for a moment to dent the Germans' confidence. In his battle report, Rommel over-dramatised and exaggerated the extent of the opposition and the scale of the fighting. The corps commanders were also concerned. At the High Command, Hitler felt that his own nervousness had been vindicated. With hindsight, one can see what a very thin film of

ABOVE General Ihler, Commander of the French IXth Corps, surrendered his troops personally to Rommel, declaring disdainfully that had there been any more ammunition he would not be standing there.

RIGHT Rommel's exhausted but exultant troops reach the sea near Fécamp.

On the quay at St Valery-en-Caux: Major-General Victor Fortune surrenders the 51st Highland Division to Rommel after a gallant defence, which Rommel was quick to acknowledge.

confidence coated the whole German direction of the invasion, and, indeed, that in mobile war, the pendulum can so easily and so swiftly swing between a strong will and a faint heart.

Rommel, however, was largely unaware of the pendulum. On 2 June, Hitler visited his division while it caught its breath. To Lu: 'The Führer's visit was wonderful. He greeted me with the words "Rommel, we were very worried about you during the attack." His whole face was radiant and I had to accompany him afterwards. I was the only divisional commander who did.'

After a few days' rest, the division swept on again. Rommel crossed the Somme. He forced the division to continue its advance across country, even those vehicles which were not

64

designed to go off the roads. To achieve more speed, he took
command of the leading battalion, but when the division
reached the Seine, he found the leading infantry milling about
with no clear plan to cross the river. He was very angry, but
once again it was he who had overreached himself, and his
division. 'I had no idea where the main body of the division
was', he wrote – an extraordinary admission from the divisional commander himself.

On 10 June, Rommel's division reached the sea west of
Dieppe, after a non-stop run of sixty miles in pursuit. The
next day, he walked into St Valery beside the leading column
of tanks to receive the British surrender. On the same day on
which Rommel's division captured St Valery, it secured its

first mention in Halder's diary, incongruously interspersed between passages during the rest of that week in which Halder was working out the way in which the German army would soon have to be reduced to a peacetime establishment now that the war was largely over. In a few days, while Rommel was still racing across northern France to the Cherbourg peninsula, Hitler was already giving Halder instructions to start reducing the army to 120 divisions from its current strength of 159.

Out in Normandy, Rommel had orders to advance as fast as he could before the armistice was signed. He covered 150 miles on 17 June before being halted south of Cherbourg. Again, the bulk of the division, struggling along behind its lightning commander, had proved unequal to the task. It took the wrong turning and was out of touch with Rommel for most of the night. For the final assault on Cherbourg, Rommel once more had to go back to the rear: 'my most important job was to get the rest of the division into action'.

Finally, on 19 June, the garrison at Cherbourg surrendered, and for Rommel the campaign was over. The division's assault on Cherbourg had been launched over a period of four days and 220 miles. To Lu: 'There were some bad moments for us and the enemy was at first between 20 and 40 times our superior in numbers. However, by buckling to quickly, we succeeded in carrying out the Führer's special order to take Cherbourg as fast as possible.' The division's casualties since 10 May were 682 killed, 1,646 wounded and 296 missing, with only 42 tanks lost. It captured 97,000 prisoners, 458 tanks and armoured cars, 4,000 lorries and several hundred guns.

'The war had turned into a lightning tour of France'

The division was then ordered south to Rennes. Rommel told Lu that the war had turned into a lightning tour of France. Halder, breaking off from a dispute with Field Marshal von Runstedt ('he uses language one would not think possible between German Generals'), had time to remark that 'fighting has ceased; now the paper work begins' – the comment of a staff officer. Rommel's perspective, as usual, was more excited and dynamic: 'At last the armistice is in force, we're now less than 200 miles from the Spanish frontier and hope to go straight there so as to get the whole Atlantic coast in our hands. How wonderful it's all been!' And then, as when he first went to war: 'Something I ate yesterday upset me, but I'm better again already. Billets middling' – the comment of a campaigning soldier.

66

4 The Desert Element

IN MARCH 1941, Italian troops in Eritrea captured a British army intelligence summary which said: 'Detachments of a German expeditionary force under an obscure German general, Rommel, have landed in North Africa.' It was already a little out of date in March 1941, since not only had the Germans landed, and Rommel with them, but they were already taking a rather more positive role than the Italian troops whom they had been sent out to join.

Rommel's historical reputation springs from his campaigns in the North African desert. The exploits of the 'Ghost Division' may have captured the imagination of the Germans through skilful use of the official information services, and probably ensured that, when Hitler was casting around for a German commander to take over in North Africa, he was quite ready to accept Rommel. But it was not until he arrived in Africa and led his joint Italian-German army up and down the desert almost incessantly for twenty-five months – always against British troops – that his reputation spread outside the confines of Nazi domestic propaganda to win for him a permanent place in the history of war.

After the fall of France, Rommel's division wintered quietly in Bordeaux with little to do even as an army of occupation. Rommel spent most of the time working on his war diary of May and June 1940, and discussing it with his staff officers. He was promoted to Lieutenant-General in January 1941, and then in early February received a summons to Berlin. After it, he wrote to Lu: 'Now I shall be able to do something for my rheumatism.' It was the nearest he could get, without breaching security, to telling her that he had been posted to Africa. He went straight to Tripoli and was to stay in Africa for more than two years.

During those years, he was twice to march fifteen hundred miles eastward up the desert into Egypt, and twice to flee fifteen hundred miles westward down it, with the British army performing the same movements in reverse. General J.C. Fuller, the military historian, explains in *The Decisive Battles of the Western World* why Libya was for so long the 'racecourse of the war' and why

... each army in turn galloped forward until its momentum was exhausted and then was compelled to gallop back to avoid annihilation. The reason centred almost entirely in supply and, like a piece of elastic, the line of supply of both armies could be stretched with comparative safety to between 300 and 400 miles from its base –

PREVIOUS PAGES German and Italian infantry pressing on in typical desert conditions. A new theatre of war: with his arrival in the desert Rommel began the greatest period of his military career.

A German tracer shell
lights up the dark
desert night.

Tripoli on the one hand and Alexandria on the other. But as these
two main bases were over 1400 miles apart, to try to stretch them
farther before intermediate bases were established was to risk
snapping the elastic. The supply problem of both sides was how to
increase the elasticity of their respective supply systems. This
could only be done by building up stockpiles at their respective
main bases and step by step pushing forward the advance bases.
As both sides were separated from their homelands by the sea, the
tussle was governed by sea communications.

Of course, the clarity of General Fuller's analysis and its
implications were often lost on both sides as they trundled
through the sand. And although the main principles explained
by him do account for the almost uncanny symmetry with
which the desert battle ebbed and flowed, there were, needless
to say, several additional factors which entered into the

71

The problem of supplies was the key to both Allied and German planning in Libya. Here a British supply convoy rattles along the narrow desert road.

equation. Along with fundamental issues of supply, there were the factors of Rommel's personality and the personalities of the British commanders who opposed him; the harassment or lack of support which all commanders received at one time or another from London and Berlin; the morale of their troops; and exhaustion, disease, pressure from allied elements, even the weather played a not inconsiderable part now and then. Then there were disparities in equipment: tanks with more or less armour plating, guns with longer range or greater armour-piercing power, anti-tank guns which stopped tanks and anti-tank guns which did not. And under it all, vast, antiseptic, cruelly naked and inhospitable, exposer of folly, wrecker of equipment, dry and still, windswept and waterlogged, with its suffocating heat and the chill of long unfriendly nights, with all these things and more, but at all times dominant – the desert, a vast sand table on which these tiny armies swirled and pirouetted like opposing fleets at sea.

Although the main supply bases at either end of the desert

were at Tripoli and Alexandria, the fighting effectively took place in an area well short of both bases, an area bounded at either end by natural bottlenecks at which the broad south-ward expanse of the desert narrows into a relative defile next to the sea, leaving a width of about forty miles before the land to the south becomes impassable to armies. In the west, this bottleneck was at El Agheila on the border between Tripoli-tania and Cyrenaica, where Rommel made his first assault in March 1941. In the east, it was at El Alamein, eighty miles west of Alexandria, where the desert fell away in a steep escarpment into the Qattara depression, about thirty miles from the coast. Between these two narrows, the desert battleground stretched out for about six hundred miles in length and at places up to one hundred miles wide. From Rommel's first position at Sirte, looking east, the coastline swept away to the north creating the bulge of northern Cyrenaica, with Benghazi at its western end and Derna at its eastern end, joined by a coast road, with other desert tracks going straight across the middle

73

through Msus, Mechili and Gazala. Fifty miles further along the coast from Gazala was Tobruk, which as a port assumed vital importance for the British advances, and which Rommel failed to capture in his first year – a failure which certainly inhibited any plans he might have had for advancing further eastward into Egypt.

Tobruk was just over a hundred miles west of the Libyan-Egyptian border, which was marked by a wide frontier fence of barbed wire entanglements which stretched southwards through the desert past Sidi Omar and Fort Maddalena. Just inside Egypt, the coast road wound through a pass at Halfaya, with natural defensive positions, and then continued virtually without interruption through Mersah Matruh, Fuka and El Alamein before ending up in Alexandria. A railway ran westward from Alexandria to the Egyptian frontier, but once in Libya – until one reached Derna – the only lines of communication were the coast road – in good order – or a variety of tracks across the desert. Most of the fighting took place on a kind of plateau which rose up in a steep escarpment from the coastal area and was negotiable in a north-south direction only at a few places.

The military geography of the desert was remarkably simple. Along its entire length there were only a few places at which troops stayed to defend fixed positions. Apart from the natural bottlenecks at either end, if one was retreating one way or the other, one would not retreat inch by inch, but go back in leaps and bounds – from Agheila to the Gazala line which provided the western defence of Tobruk; from Gazala to the Sollum/Bardia line on the frontier; from there to the base area at Mersah Matruh. Between these places there was no position to defend, and there were few airstrips to enable one to bring any appreciable tactical air power to bear on the battle. The desert campaigns were basically a war of manœuvre between accepted fixed points up and down the sand table.

So this was Rommel's element. Between his arrival in Africa in February 1941 and his final departure in March 1943, Rommel's campaigns can be divided into four distinct periods – advance, retreat, advance, retreat.

In the first phase, he was in the ascendant from March 1941 until November 1941. He pushed the British back from their positions threatening Tripolitania, and advanced as far as the frontier with Egypt. Then, in November 1941, phase two

OPPOSITE A German soldier gazes through his periscope across the vast wasteland at the distant enemy.

74

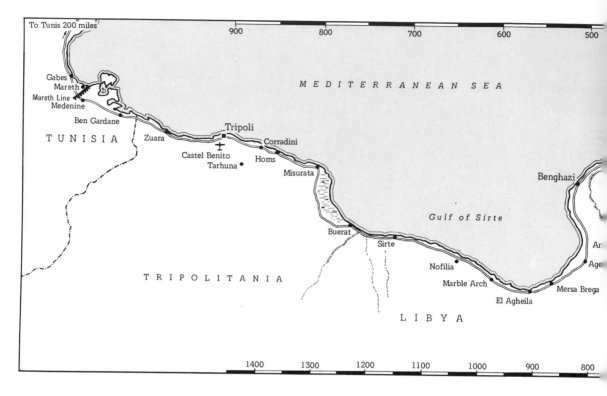

opened with a tactical defeat in the battle called 'Crusader', and the first retreat began. By the time it ended, he was virtually back where he had started. Phase three replaced phase two almost before the latter was really finished. In January 1942, Rommel performed a lightning turn round, and converted his retreat into another advance, which this time took him, by May, to the Gazala line, by June to the capture of Tobruk, by July into Egypt and to the El Alamein defence line at which he was finally brought to a halt at the first battle of that name. There was then a pause while both sides found their breath. Phase four opened up at the end of October 1942, with the second battle of El Alamein. Rommel was dislodged from his defensive positions and forced into a continuous retreat which did not stop until he reached Tunisia the following March, more than fifteen hundred miles to the rear. When he left Africa that month for good, with his largely broken and and surrounded army behind him, the Axis cause in Africa was virtually at an end.

It is doubtful, however, whether any such dramatic and disastrous developments were anticipated by Hitler and the German general staff when they chose to send Rommel to

76

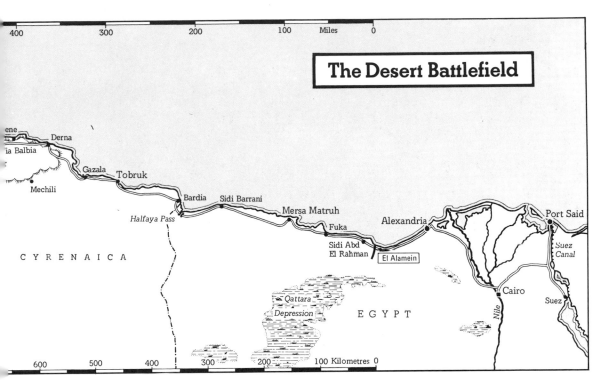

The Desert Battlefield

Africa in early 1941. The desert war had started in September 1940, when Graziani, the Italian commander, pushed his divisions into Egypt against virtually non-existent British defences, and soon reached Sidi Barrani. There he started to consolidate his position. This gave the British time to prepare a counter-attack which was duly launched in early December 1940. About thirty thousand British troops were sent in against the Italian army, which numbered – in the forward areas alone – nearly three times their strength. By 8 February, when Rommel was in Berlin, the British army had taken Tobruk, forced the Italians out of Cyrenaica, captured nearly 130,000 prisoners and was occupying El Agheila in a position threatening Tripolitania. Rommel later noted in his diary that if Wavell, the British Commander-in-Chief in Cairo, had continued his advance into Tripolitania, no resistance worthy of the name could have been put up against him. The Italian army in Africa had almost ceased to exist. In fact, Wavell was prevented from exploiting his victory by the decision of the British Cabinet to divert many of his troops from the North African theatre to the defence of Greece.

Although it has been argued that Wavell, if unhindered by

Italian troops captured in the British advance through Eritrea are shipped out from Tobruk to prison camps behind the lines.

the short-lived and disastrous plan to send troops to Greece, could have sent his army commander, General O'Connor, another six hundred miles on to capture Tripoli, Churchill turned the plan down in favour of Greece. Indeed, he went further: he cajoled Wavell with the vast numbers of men on the ration strength of Middle East Command who could not be 'rowing their weight in the boat', and, in a fit of fury one night at a defence committee meeting, railed at the Chiefs-of-Staff that 'it was not more troops that Wavell needed out there, but firing squads and courts martial'.

So, at the time at which Rommel arrived, his opposing commander was experiencing just that lack of interest and support which he himself was destined to suffer from Berlin for most of his time in Africa. The question is, however, had he ever been led to expect anything else? The British Cabinet after the Greek fiasco soon returned to the view that the Libyan campaign was, for Britain, the vital strategic engagement, worthy of all the time and military resources that could be applied to it. For the High Command in Berlin, however, the Africa campaign, certainly at its inception – and perhaps really for its duration, was a sideshow designed as a holding

78

operation, originally conceived to prevent the Italians from being forced out of Africa.

When Rommel answered his summons to Berlin on 6 February, he was told that on account of the Italians' critical situation in Africa, a German Africa Corps was to be formed with two German divisions – one light and one Panzer – and was to be sent to Libya to help Graziani. Rommel was to be the corps commander and was to move off immediately. The first German troops would arrive by mid-February, the 5th Light Division by mid-April and the Panzer Division by the end of May. Ominously for Rommel, he was also told that, though he would be in command of the Italian motorised elements, he would be subordinate to the Italian Commander-in-Chief, Marshal Graziani. His command relationships with the Italians were destined to create endless trouble for Rommel in the two years in which he was in Africa.

After receiving these instructions from the German Commander-in-Chief, Field Marshal von Brauchitsch, Rommel went to see Hitler in the afternoon and Halder the following morning. Hitler told him that he had been recommended as the man who could most quickly adapt himself to the unknown conditions of desert warfare. But apart from these pleasantries, what were Hitler's real intentions in sending Rommel to Africa? As it turned out, Rommel's genius on the battlefield, and his distance from Berlin, enabled him so to transform the situation he found in Africa, and to create there a whole new range of possibilities for German strategy, that he assumed that his leaders in Berlin would also revise their original evaluation of the relative unimportance of his mission. In this he was mistaken. They never really did so, except under the occasional and temporary influence of a particularly spectacular victory by the Africa Corps.

Throughout Rommel's time in Africa, and for months even before he went out there, the whole weight of German military preoccupation had been concentrated on the preparations for the gigantic attack on Russia – Operation Barbarossa – which was to be launched in June 1941. Week after week, Halder's diary is full of massive planning operations involving staff work on a quite unprecedented scale. In contrast, we find him noting on 16 January that, 'The war in Africa need not bother us very much. Even now the military situation is better than a year ago, but we must not risk the internal collapse of Italy. Italy must be saved from that. It will be necessary to send

BELOW Field Marshal Wavell, in Rommel's opinion the most gifted of the British commanders in Africa. His opinion was not shared by Churchill.

79

Relations between Rommel and his Italian allies left much to be desired. This scene on a landing strip at the Libyan front shows Rommel typically distant from the Italian Generals.

some help.' Halder told Rommel, therefore, that his main task was to see that Graziani did not retreat the remaining five hundred miles from Sirte to Tripoli without a fight. He was asked to send in a staff appreciation from Rome after speaking to the Italian High Command, and to keep in touch with General Paulus, one of Halder's assistants.

A month later, on 10 March, Rommel was told by the OKH (the German supreme army command) not to advance too far until the 5th Division arrived. On 11 March, he flew home to report to Hitler and his generals. He told them that the British position in the bulge of Benghazi offered favourable conditions for him to carry out a successful attack. He would not be able to attack further eastwards, towards Tobruk, until he had dislodged the British forces from their positions along the Jebel Akhdar, which stretched from Benghazi to Derna at the northern end of the bulge. It was agreed between them, and von Brauchitsch repeated to Rommel, that they did not believe that the Africa Corps was yet strong enough to undertake major operations, but should start to prepare for a drive on Tobruk the following autumn. The OKH then turned its mind to its other operations in Finland, Rumania, Albania, Greece,

Norway, Algiers and Yugoslavia – and, of course, the ever-dominant planning for Barbarossa.

One can see what Rommel had to contend with in his superiors, but one can also see what Halder and the OKH had to contend with in Rommel. Even allowing for the great difficulties created by the very different temperaments of Halder and Rommel, they were clearly from the very first meeting talking two totally different languages born from almost diametrically opposite perspectives. Halder was to become obsessed with the Russian venture; yet Rommel was not milk-white either. We shall see also his increasing incapacity to appreciate that his own part in German grand strategy was, at that stage, only minor. How exasperating it must have been for him to advance across hundreds of miles, and apparently overturn all the accepted strategic premises in the Middle East, without these implications making any impact on those obsessive 'Barbarossans' in Berlin! But this is one of the main paradoxes of Rommel's life. He had been born and reared in the rigid orthodoxy of the Second Reich. Here he was now, a man whose behaviour between the wars suggests that he had been faithfully inculcated with the virtues of obedience to authority, and of the subordination of tactics to the grand strategy, yet who repeatedly failed to see that, however spectacular his victories in the desert and however imaginative his plans for exploiting them, German strategy at the time was ineluctably caught up in the Russian operation; and that campaign had a momentum and a scale which would have required more than the victories of two enterprising German divisions in the North African sideshow to alter its course. It may have been shortsighted of the Halders and the Hitlers as they peered obsessively at their maps of the Ukraine, but in terms of their original instructions to Rommel, one can hardly accuse them of letting him down. The young subaltern in Rommel's company who had advanced too far in the Carpathians twenty-five years earlier had received short shrift and no help from Rommel when he appealed for it. It was a bitter lesson for Rommel the Field Marshal to have to relearn himself.

When Rommel arrived in Tripoli on 12 February 1941, he found the Italians' morale at rock bottom after the enormous defeats which they had received at the hands of O'Connor. He also found that Graziani had given up the Italian High Command in Africa and had been succeeded by his Chief-of-Staff, General Garibaldi. From the start, Rommel was impatient

'In Tripoli Rommel found the Italians' morale at rock bottom'

81

A sandstorm near Bir el
Harmat envelops German
troops of the 90th Light
Division in a choking blanket
of grit. A pastel sketch by
Wilhelm Wessel.

with his Italian allies and lacked confidence in their Command.

He decided to take over immediate command at the front, ignoring the advice that he had received to confine his visit to an initial reconnaissance and wait until the German units arrived. On his first afternoon in Tripoli, he flew forward to Sirte to inspect the terrain and the meagre Italian defences round the village. He decided immediately that the Sirte position must be defended properly, but found that there was no

Allied troops against the Classical ruins of Cyrene, the ancient milestone halfway between Benghazi and Tobruk.

more than a single Italian regiment in the vicinity, the remaining Italian formations being two hundred miles to the rear – halfway back towards Tripoli. However, on 14 February, three days after his own arrival, Rommel was relieved to witness the first German units starting to disembark. They consisted of a reconnaissance battalion and an anti-tank battalion – not much, but in the prevailing climate of insecurity in Tripoli, they were clearly more than welcome.

Tripoli, February 1941: the newly arrived Rommel reviews his troops
in the main square; the parade was intended to impress the local
population and the Allies with a spurious show of strength.

Because Rommel was still unaware of the recent British decision to divert resources to Greece – he became aware of it only after a week or so – his first days were spent arranging measures to obscure what he thought was the basic weakness of his position and to bluff what he imagined were the still overwhelming British forces into believing that a substantial Axis reinforcement was in progress. In those early days, Rommel literally commuted every morning from Tripoli to Sirte, flying back in the evening for a round trip of seven hundred miles. He started to plan a counter-offensive at the moment at which his early patrols told him that his fears of an imminent British attack were unfounded. On their side, the British appear to have had little awareness of the aggressive commander now facing them. On 19 February, Wavell, in Cairo, wrote an appreciation which argued that there was at that stage no serious risk of an Axis counter-attack in Cyrenaica. Moreover, even after his own staff, a few weeks later, had worked out a dummy appreciation, putting themselves in Rommel's shoes and assuming a successful recapture of Cyrenaica, the implications were not generally accepted. Admittedly, had Wavell and his advisers been privy to Rommel's sessions with Hitler, von Brauchitsch and Halder on 19 March, they would have felt their confidence vindicated. But they would have been reckoning without Rommel, as indeed the German High Command in Berlin appeared to do too. Rommel left Berlin distressed at the OKH efforts to keep down the number of his troops and to 'leave the future of this theatre of war to chance'. If that was what they intended to do, then one can imagine his resolving to play a decisive part in shaping that chance, if necessary with only the few troops he then had, until by his actions with them he could convince his masters of the case for more.

Even before he had gone to Berlin, he had ordered his 5th Light Division to attack El Agheila on 24 March, and this attack was duly, and successfully, accomplished. The El Agheila assault was not intended to be the beginning of a major campaign, but once he had started, Rommel soon found that he could not stop. Warfare was to him something more like a continuous operation than a series of set-piece attacks. It was a dynamic and unpredictable process in which the only hope of any kind of mastery was to keep moving. So, six days after the El Agheila assault, he ordered another reconnaissance in force to Mersa Brega, forty miles farther on. General

Neame, the British commander who had succeeded O'Connor, was ordered to withdraw. General Wavell told him that his task for the next two months was to prevent Rommel from crossing the 150 miles between El Agheila and Benghazi, without incurring heavy losses to the British armour and motorised units. In the event, Rommel was in Benghazi in a few days, Neame was a prisoner and his armoured forces were scattered over the desert well to the rear.

From Mersa Brega, Rommel went straight on to surround Agedabia. In his diaries, one senses the same atmosphere of dynamism and constant movement which characterised his narrative of the French invasion nearly a year before. Of course, there are differences: instead of the divisional commander carrying out his forward reconnaissance on foot, and travelling up and down his divisional area in an armoured car, we now see the corps commander flying everywhere in a little Storch spotter aircraft. Where, in France, fifty miles was an exceptional leap for his division, here the Africa Corps is already strung out over desert distances twice or three times as long. One thing about Rommel's campaign which never changed, however, was his capacity to become exposed to

German armour being unloaded at Tripoli harbour.

Rommel inspecting the captured fortress of El Agheila, April 1941.

personal danger, and his equally good fortune in escaping from that danger. Near Agedabia, his plane was fired on, at a height of only 150 feet, by Italian troops who had never seen a Storch before. Another time, he was caught in a sandstorm, and only the refusal of the pilot to be bullied by Rommel into flying on saved them both from flying into death.

By 3 April, ten days after the first move, Rommel's personal air reconnaissance had given him enough evidence to conclude that a major British retreat was in hand. He decided to re-capture the whole of Cyrenaica. Indeed, his thoughts were already reaching much farther than that. One evening, in his tent, upon hearing the bad news from the Eritrean campaign, he laughed and told his staff officers: 'We shall reach the Nile, make a right turn and win back everything.'

As the speed of the advance started to quicken, two things happened to Rommel which typified the highly idiosyncratic and personal nature of his command of the Africa Corps. Near Mechili, his Storch landed in a sandhill and could not take off again. He narrowly escaped capture by an approaching British column only by taking flight in a discarded German truck which he found in the vicinity. The other event, which was a direct consequence of the first, was that he was completely out of contact with his headquarters – indeed with his entire army. No one knew where he was or where to find him. There was thus a certain amount of confusion between Rommel's original orders for the newly-arrived 5th Light Division to advance on Mechili, and new orders from his staff who felt that the situation had developed promisingly enough to justify by-passing Mechili in a leapfrog movement straight to Tobruk. When Rommel reappeared, he declared angrily that he had personally visited the 5th Light Division headquarters and confirmed his original order to attack Mechili. But his anger could not obscure the fact that the corps had been forced to operate for some time in a fast-moving mobile battle without its commander, who might easily have come to the same decision to go straight to Tobruk had he remained in a central position at which he could more competently assess the overall situation. Had he done so, he might well have reached Tobruk in time to prevent the British defences consolidating. As it was, the British had time to build up Tobruk, and Rommel's subsequent failure to capture it in 1941 prevented him from a much longer eastward advance.

In fairness to Rommel, he was not the only general in the desert hurrying about out of touch with troops and headquarters. The North African campaign was singular for the number of generals who were captured simply because sharp battlelines were so seldom drawn, and because each engagement resembled nothing so much as a general mêlée over a very large area. On the night of 6 April, Generals Neame and O'Connor got lost together in their staff car and were captured by a German recce group as they drove north from Mechili to Derna, hoping to make contact with the British units which were trapped in Derna. When Rommel drove into Mechili the next day, he found O'Connor's armoured command vehicle, the Mammoth, lying abandoned but otherwise intact, even to the provision of a pair of sun- and sand-goggles. He climbed into the vehicle and put on the goggles saying: 'Booty – permissible, I take it, even for a general.' The goggles and the Mammoth were to become an inseparable part of Rommel's image during the next two years.

By 10 April, Rommel had reached the outer defences of Tobruk, and there he was brought to a halt for the first time. However, in the space of just over two weeks, what he called 'an unprepared offensive' had driven the British out of western

Cyrenaica and had reversed the strategic situation which had obtained in North Africa when he arrived. Naturally, it was not entirely his own doing, but Rommel's genius in the desert was his exploitation of every offensive opportunity that presented itself to him, however small, in the hope of acquiring such momentum that his innate confidence in victory would become, in a sense, self-fulfilling. Indeed, from his point of view, the victories in those two weeks had the desired effect on the British.

Wavell was certainly taken by surprise by the speed and success of Rommel's offensive. He had not believed that an enemy offensive was really possible until May, and in this he was objectively right, if one assumed that, to be effective, the offensive needed the supplies and reinforcements which had not even started to arrive when Rommel began his advance eastward. But Wavell also found that in Neame he had chosen the wrong man to succeed O'Connor. When, after a week of fighting, the fall of Benghazi was imminent, Wavell became convinced that Neame had lost control of the situation, and he wanted to go to the front and assert his own authority over the battle. History might then have changed direction, but, incredibly, there was no suitable aircraft available for Wavell to travel in, and his journey was delayed. When he finally got to Tobruk, a week later, the situation was much more out of hand. Wavell too was nearly captured on his return to Cairo: his plane had to make a forced landing and the Commander-in-Chief of the entire African and Middle East theatre was

German infantry encircling Mersa Brega, one of the prizes in Rommel's bewilderingly rapid advance from El Agheila to Benghazi in the spring of 1941.

A German soldiers' cinema in captured Benghazi.

saved from falling into the hands of the advancing Germans only by a lone Sudanese soldier who turned up in a single truck and drove him to safety.

Rommel was indeed fortunate to have as his opposing Commander-in-Chief a man whose time and energy during those critical weeks were almost entirely taken up with the rapidly-developing disaster in Greece and Crete. Indeed, throughout the two years in which Rommel was in the desert, there was a striking contrast between the relative independence of his own command – subject of course to the stringent supply shortages from which he later suffered – and in particular his freedom to concentrate entirely on the desert battle in front of him, and the incessant, multifarious and very much more strategic preoccupations affecting an enormous theatre of operations which continuously beset the British Commander-in-Chief in Cairo. Yet each time that his opposing Commander-in-Chief – both Wavell and his successor Auchinleck – got up from his desk in Cairo and came down to fight Rommel face-to-face, Rommel's dominance of the battle was no longer assured.

As Rommel approached Tobruk in early April, Wavell just

had time to fly up to Tobruk and pull the British forces together to stop the helter-skelter slide back into Egypt. He decided to make Tobruk into a fortress, with the main British defence line farther east at Sollum. Then he was off to Athens. While three unsuccessful German assaults were being repulsed from Tobruk, Wavell was coping with the deteriorating Greek campaign, which ended in Greece's capitulation to the Germans on 24 April, and the evacuation of those precious British troops who had been diverted from the Cyrenaica campaign only a few months before. In Cairo, the situation appeared to have grim possibilities. The general staff dusted out its files on the 'worst possible case' of Rommel breaking through to the Nile. These plans had first been postulated a year earlier, when the Italians captured Sidi Barrani. But, as is usual with contingency plans, their significance was exaggerated outside the headquarters, and Churchill never really forgave Wavell for the defeatism which he believed was implicit in this contemplation of the unmentionable. Indeed, once again he lost his temper at the mere suggestion that Egypt might be lost, and told his army chiefs that, 'if Wavell lost Egypt, blood would flow and he would have firing parties to shoot the generals'.

Ironically, while Wavell in adversity was getting into trouble with London, Rommel in victory was in almost as much bother with Berlin. In fact, though it would not be true to say that it was Rommel's victories which were upsetting Berlin, the German general staff were clearly reluctant to make any further provision for the Africa Corps, whatever its successes, if this would jeopardise the final preparations for Barbarossa. Rommel had hardly reached the outskirts of Tobruk before Halder was referring to his 'preposterous demands'. After Rommel's forces had again been repulsed from Tobruk, Halder drily notes: 'Rommel has at last admitted that his forces are not strong enough to take full advantage of the unique opportunities. It is the impression we have had for some time.' A week later, he is at Rommel again:

OVERLEAF Tobruk harbour, smashed by bombing, scene of the departure for captivity of many Allied and Axis prisoners. This pastel sketch by Wilhelm Wessel was drawn after the capture of Tobruk by the German forces, June 1942.

The reports from North Africa worry me. Rommel has not reported, but I feel things are in a mess. Reports from officers show that he is in no way up to his operational task. All day long he rushes about between widely scattered units. He fritters away his forces in reconnaissance raids and piecemeal thrusts of weak armoured forces which are costly. Our air transport cannot meet his senseless demands. Aircraft landing there find no fuel for the return flight.

93

Tobruk nach der Einnahme
22.6.42

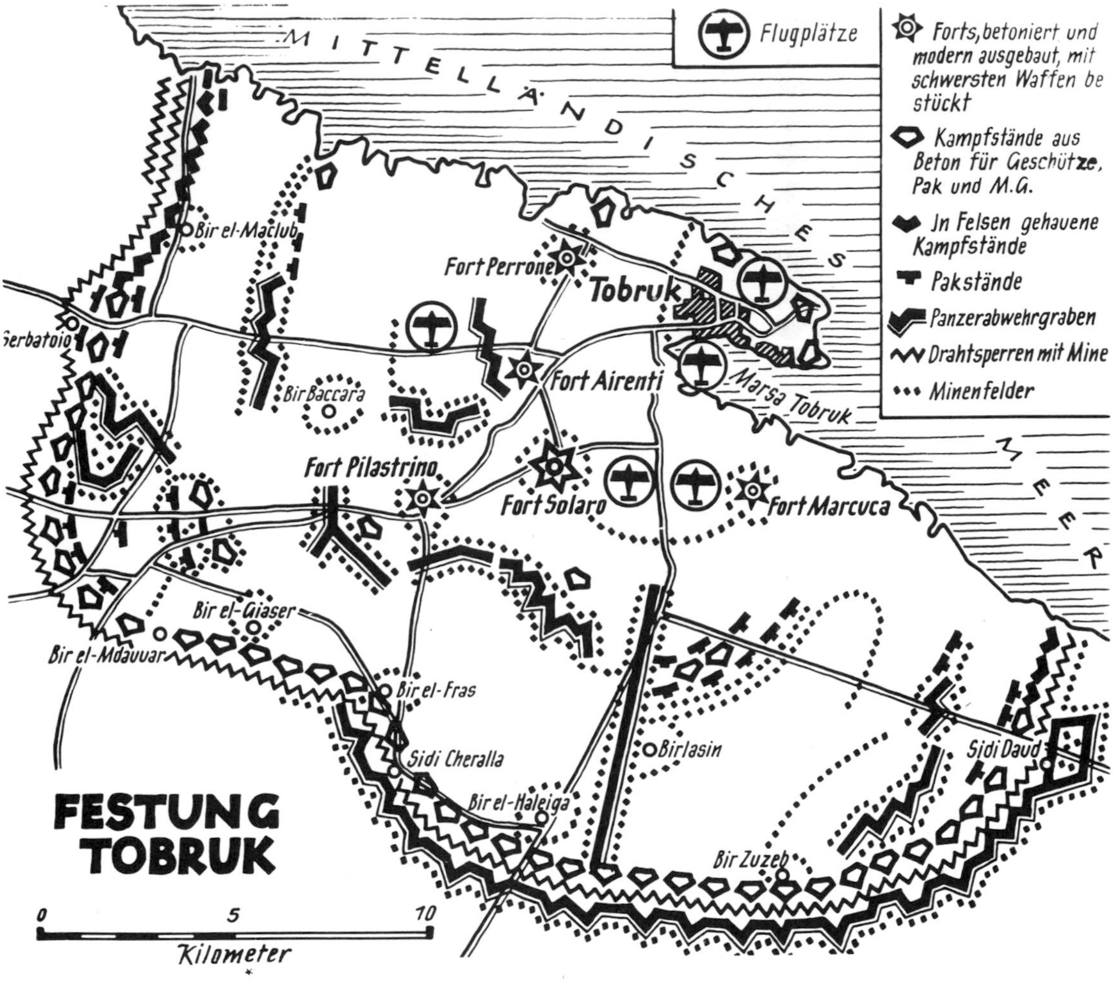
MITTELLÄNDISCHES
MEER
Flugplätze
Forts, betoniert und modern ausgebaut, mit schwersten Waffen be stückt
Kampfstände aus Beton für Geschütze, Pak und M.G.
Jn Felsen gehauene Kampfstände
Pakstände
Panzerabwehrgraben
Drahtsperren mit Mine
Minenfelder
Bir el-Maclub
Fort Perrone
Tobruk
Fort Airenti
Marsa Tobruk
Bir Baccara
Fort Pilastrino
Fort Solaro
Fort Marcuca
Bir el-Giaser
Bir el-Mdauuar
Bir el-Fras
Sidi Cheralla
Bir el-Haleiga
Birlasin
Bir Zuzeb
Sidi Daud
FESTUNG
TOBRUK
0
5
10
Kilometer

A German map of the British defences at Tobruk, listing in the following order: concrete forts with heavy artillery; concrete anti-tank and machine gun posts; emplacements hollowed out of the rock; anti-tank gun emplacements; tank-traps; mined barbed-wire barriers; minefields.

Should he go out to make an on-the-spot assessment? No, Halder concluded; but decided instead to send out General Paulus as 'perhaps the only man with enough personal influence to head off this soldier gone stark mad'.

What had gone wrong? Two factors were really at work. One was the crescendo of preparation for Barbarossa, which was due to start in just under two months' time. The other was the fact that, basically, the German general staff did not want to be bothered by the Africa campaign. They had sent Rommel out there to get on with it with a certain number of troops. If he did anything which required more troops, they would be basically rather irritated, even if, as it turned out, his demand for reinforcements derived from the greater opportunities which he had exposed, rather than because the troops they had originally allocated to him were unequal to the task he had been given.

In fact, the OKH reluctantly agreed to send Rommel five more battalions, and to improve the supply organisation through Naples. Halder's assessment was that a decisive attack on Tobruk was out of the question, and Rommel came to the same conclusion about ten days later. Should the siege of Tobruk be raised, and Rommel withdraw from his positions at Sollum a hundred miles farther east? Halder recognised the political undesirability of this course, but told Paulus, prior to his visit, to impress on Rommel that resources were slender, that no more help could be forthcoming and that if he could not maintain his present position in those circumstances, he must make the necessary adjustments. Even Hitler was taking a cautious view. If Tobruk fell, he instructed Rommel to advance only as far as the Sollum/Bardia line, to consolidate there and to make only reconnaissance forays deeper into Egypt – even if the enemy withdrew farther. If the British held out in Tobruk (as indeed they did), then Rommel should withdraw to a defensive line about forty miles to the west at Gazala.

A few days later, Paulus radioed his report from North Africa. The Tobruk assault was over, he said, and Rommel's troops were in bad shape. He had instructed Rommel to hold Cyrenaica at all costs and to construct a firm defensive line. Above all, the crux was neither Sollum nor Tobruk, but supply. He then returned to Berlin and reported personally to Halder while Rommel's 'distress calls became more urgent'.

Rommel passing on his instructions by field telephone: his erratic communications sometimes earned him strong criticism from High Command.

Rommel's Element

One thing about Rommel's campaigns which
never changed was his capacity to become
exposed to personal danger, and his good fortune
in escaping from that danger. Compared to
France, where his forward reconnaissances were
made on foot, the Divisional Commander in
Africa had to travel up and down much larger
areas, sometimes in armoured cars, sometimes in
a little Storch spotter aircraft.

BELOW Rommel rapidly
made the desert his element,
racing ahead of his troops
with characteristic audacity.

RIGHT Rommel about to
take off for a reconnaissance
flight in his Fiesler Storch
spotter plane.

FAR RIGHT Rommel eating
from a tin of the German
soldiers' rations. These tins
were often stamped A.M.,
which the troops understood
to mean *Alter Mann* (old
man). They regarded
captured bully beef as a
rare delicacy.

Halder concluded that Rommel, 'by overstepping his orders has brought about a situation for which our present supplies are insufficient. Rommel cannot cope with the situation.' As it happened, he was wrong, but there was one outcome of the Paulus visit which no German could predict. It had a galvanising effect on the British.

This quite unpredictable consequence arose because Paulus's first cable to Berlin was intercepted and decoded in London. Churchill reacted instantly. He cabled to Wavell urging him to take advantage of the weaknesses in Rommel's situation which had been so helpfully exposed for him by General Paulus. Wavell must retake the offensive, he said, as soon as he received the three hundred tanks which were then already on their way in convoy through the Mediterranean. On 15 May, without waiting for the tanks, Wavell instructed one of his corps commanders, General Gott, to attack Rommel in the Sollum area. The British captured Sollum and Capuzzo momentarily, but then Rommel counter-attacked and the British withdrew from all their newly-won positions except the Halfaya Pass, and retreated even from there a few days later, under the impact of a renewed attack by Rommel. Churchill's pressure on Wavell continued. Rommel, meanwhile, consolidated his positions round Halfaya, and round the perimeter which kept the Tobruk garrison from breaking out behind his front line. Eventually, Wavell was reluctantly forced, against his instincts, into planning Operation 'Battleaxe' for 15 June.

Wavell's plan for the battle was to be based on a three-pronged attack against Rommel's forces. The first prong, between the coast and the high escarpment, would advance on and capture Sollum barracks. The second column, on top of the escarpment and to the south of it, was to advance to Halfaya and Capuzzo, while the third column, consisting of most of the armour, was to keep farther south and, by threatening to sweep round Rommel's right flank and attack his rear and his supply lines, lure his armour into a tank battle in the open desert south of Capuzzo or Halfaya. If Rommel then withdrew into Bardia, Wavell intended to press on to El Adam, and ultimately to join up with the garrison at Tobruk, but that second phase would have to depend on how the first part of the battle progressed.

Rommel, for his part, intended to let any British offensive just wear itself out on the by now well-prepared anti-tank defensive positions. He hoped virtually to keep the powder dry in his two armoured formations, holding them in the rear for later committal as the battle developed. His army was poised rather like a dancer ready to sway or swivel in any direction. Perhaps this is how Rommel himself saw it, because he later described how 'in a decisive moment it is often possible to decide the issue by making an unexpected shift of one's main weight'. On the third day of Battleaxe, that is just what he did.

The first day of the British attack found Rommel well prepared, in both the Halfaya and Capuzzo areas. No great British headway was made at Halfaya, though the centre column succeeded during the first afternoon in taking Capuzzo and then turning right-handed towards Sollum and the sea. One of the most serious factors affecting early British tank losses was the devastating use made by the Germans of their 88 mm anti-aircraft guns converted into an anti-tank role. However, the British plan for the second day was to continue slogging on. Rommel meanwhile decided to commit his two armoured formations to the battle, having decided that the British armour had by then been satisfactorily worn down on his defences. As it turned out, he was half wrong. When the 15th Panzer Division was sent into battle in the Capuzzo area, it made little headway and eventually, towards

British gun carriers in the heavily-shelled ruins of Fort Capuzzo.

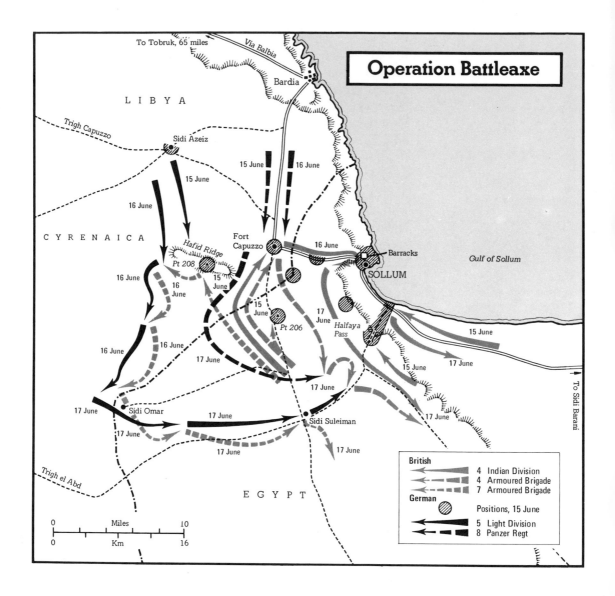

Operation Battleaxe

British
4 Indian Division
4 Armoured Brigade
7 Armoured Brigade
German
Positions, 15 June
5 Light Division
8 Panzer Regt

the end of the second day, had to disengage. The 5th Light Division, however, some sixteen miles farther west, succeeded in overcoming the British brigade opposing it and continued its advance towards Sidi Suleiman, some eight to ten miles to the rear of Britain's forward position in the fight round Capuzzo.

It was at this point, on the second night of the three-day battle, that Rommel decided to shift his weight. In doing so, he achieved a decisive change in his fortunes. Until that moment, the battle of attrition of the first two days had, on balance, probably ended better for the British than for the Germans. Certainly, that was what the British felt on the second night, and Rommel too knew that the 15th Panzer Division's tank strength had dropped from eighty to thirty. But Rommel's subsequent manœuvres managed to take the British by surprise, throw them off balance and cause a hasty withdrawal, leaving Rommel in sole possession of the battle-field.

Retaining only enough units in the Capuzzo area to pin down the British front, he disengaged the rest of the 15th Panzer Division from the battle and wheeled them round in a wide right-handed arc to join forces with the 5th Light Division, which was by then coming in from the wings and threatening the British rear at Sidi Suleiman. With the German forces thus concentrated, the British commanders had barely enough time to withdraw across the enemy's front before Rommel bore down on them.

By the afternoon of 17 June, it was all over. Wavell, who had flown up too late to see for himself, returned to Cairo and opened his signal to London with the words: 'I regret to report the failure of Battleaxe.' Rommel and the Africa Corps were exultant. To Lu, Rommel wrote of 'a complete victory'. He spent three days going round the battlefield and then wrote again, 'Now the enemy can come, he'll get an even bigger beating.' Even Halder could scarce forbear to cheer from his usually cheerless office at the OKH. 'Losses at Sollum', he wrote, 'are 560 – reasonable, and a better proportion than at Tobruk.' He then turned to his Barbarossa calculations – German divisions in the field, 141; Russian, 213. In a few days' time, in the Russian theatre, he was to start calculating losses in hundreds of thousands, but of Africa all he could say was that 560 was reasonable. In London, Churchill, if not inconsolable, nevertheless resolved to change his commanders. On 21 June, the day on which Hitler attacked Russia, Wavell was replaced by Auchinleck. With his victory in Battleaxe, Rommel's first phase in Africa was virtually over. It was to be some months before the new phase began.

'I regret to report the failure of Battleaxe'

5 Back to Square One

FROM JUNE UNTIL NOVEMBER 1941, the desert war saw a period of consolidation and reorganisation on both sides. While the first weeks of the enormous German offensive against Russia were in progress, Rommel clearly had little chance of attracting much attention from anybody at OKH or the supreme combined headquarters, OKW. The North African entries in Halder's diaries stand out like tiny sentinels in a vast array of notes on the movement of men and materials across western Russia. But when they do occur, they show Halder to be still dedicated to the derogation of Rommel and indeed of the whole African campaign as it was affecting the overall German strategy.

One of the main disputes during the summer concerned the command structure of the African forces, which were eventually reorganised from being merely the Africa Corps to becoming the Panzer Group Africa. Rommel – newly promoted to Panzer General – was put in command of the army group which consisted of both the Africa Corps and five Italian divisions. Halder and von Brauchitsch had also sent out General Gause with a large independent staff of his own to act as liaison officer with the Italians in Africa. This was probably a ruse to contain Rommel's excesses, and perhaps also to mitigate the ill-feeling which appeared to be endemic between Rommel and his Italian colleagues. However, Rommel soon sorted it out to his satisfaction. After a talk with Gause at this time, Halder notes that personal relations at the headquarters were 'complicated by Rommel's character and inordinate ambition. Mutual confidence between Rommel and Gause has not been established.' 'Rommel's character defects', he continued, 'make him hard to get on with, but no-one cares to come out into the open because of his brutality and his top level backing.' Armed with this self-same top-level backing in the form of Hitler, Rommel had in fact deliberately ignored the OKH instructions to Gause not to place himself under Rommel's command, and had told Gause categorically that the command of all troops in Africa was vested in him alone, and that Gause would be his Chief-of-Staff in the army group but would have no independent status. Though Rommel never in his life showed any aspirations to social status outside his military world, on questions of military status which also affected command functions – as was usually the case – no one would fight harder for position than he. To Lu at the time he wrote: 'I'm very pleased about my new

PREVIOUS PAGES Chief of Staff, General Gause (right), was entrusted by the German High Command with the task of smoothing relations between Rommel and the Italians. Behind Rommel is General Navarini.

appointment. Everybody else in that position [in command of an army group] is a Colonel General. If things go here as I should like them to, I too will probably get that rank after the war's over.' And then, a little later, as though to confound Halder's secret thoughts of the month before, 'I'm getting along famously with my new chief of staff [General Gause].'

Meanwhile, the supply situation was continuing to worry Germans on both sides of the Mediterranean. Early in August, Halder notes that it would be a 'crime' to allocate German planes to the defence of the Italian-German supply route across the Mediterranean, yet in the same week, he goes on to make provision for a decision by Hitler to send Rommel 350 new tank engines all the way by air. In September, Hitler approves a paper which says that the German-Italian position in Libya will become increasingly difficult unless supplies are stepped up or unless Rommel takes Tobruk (impossible until October, Halder notes in the margin). The successful arrival at Benghazi of one shipment stirs Rommel to write to Lu: 'It took 50 hours to unload. You can imagine how pleased I was. With things as they are in the Mediterranean, it's not easy to

German Junker fighters over Mt Etna, escorting an air convoy to North Africa on one of the rare occasions when air power was allocated to meet Rommel's need. The German supply situation became more and more desperate as ever fewer vessels got through by the Mediterranean route.

Rommel with General Garibaldi (right) at a victory parade. Rommel had no faith in the Italian command, who, in turn, accused him of arrogance and overweening ambition.

get anything across. For the moment we're only stepchildren and must make the best of it.' Characteristically, he ended this letter on the subject of food: 'Gruenther [his batman] is doing fried potatoes this evening which I'm looking forward to after being off my food for a few days.'

The desert routine during those summer months must have been concerned as much with the numerous little fights at the domestic and personal level as with the much larger fight against the British. The heat, the food and the flies all conspired to narrow one's horizons and to concentrate most of one's energies on the immediate struggle not so much to survive as to survive in some degree of comfort. Lu must have become used to the minutiae of desert life: 'A quite atrocious heat even during the night, one lies tossing and turning and dripping with sweat. . . . My bed is now standing in tins filled with water and I hope the nights will be a little more restful from now on. . . . It's so hot one steams even early in the morning.' Then there were the bugs: 'Bagged two bugs. . . . Liquid-

108

Rommel decorating Italian
soldiers while men of the
Africa Corps look on.
Despite his scornful attitude,
even Rommel admitted that
individually, the Italians
were capable of
great heroism.

ated four bugs. . . . Unfortunately the bugs are still about . . .
but I hope to win this campaign also. . . . I've been free of
bugs ever since I had petrol poured over my wire bedstead and
set light to it.' And the food – Rommel made a point of eating
the same food as his men, and noted with disfavour that the
Italian officers were accustomed to have quite different food
from their men. But the 'perpetual mush' did not much appeal
to his tender stomach, and his letters to Lu over the months
are a veritable litany of gastric discomfort.

One day, for a treat, he and his staff had fresh liver, from
a gazelle shot by Rommel during a hunting expedition with
Major von Mellethin and Lieutenant Schmidt, two members
of the staff. According to Schmidt, Rommel was nearly beside
himself with excitement during the chase. Armed with a service rifle and a submachine-gun, they tore across the desert
in two cars after a herd of gazelle. Each time the herd split into
two, Rommel swerved after the larger group until he had
whittled it down to just three gazelles. The pace got faster and

faster, the bumps more pronounced, the swerves round rocks and boulders wilder. Eventually, Rommel came up to his quarry, stood up in his car and fired his submachine gun. A gazelle dropped. Rommel, in a hitherto unexpected role as far as his staff were concerned, leaped out of the car armed with a hunting knife, skilfully eviscerated the gazelle and sawed off its horns to take back as a trophy.

Of course, life was not all gazelle- or bug-hunting. As the months went by, it became more and more obvious to Rommel that his position was basically untenable as long as the British held out in Tobruk behind his forward lines and threatening his lines of communication, which stretched back three hundred miles to Benghazi and nearly a thousand miles to Tripoli. He could certainly not advance farther, while Tobruk remained in British hands; nor could he afford to wait where he was until the British launched their next attack; and retreat was unthinkable. His autumn plan thus centred on the need to capture Tobruk, and throughout September and October he

Rommel's advance headquarters near Tobruk: a photograph taken from Rommel's own Storch aircraft. Unlike the Italian Generals, who often lived in great luxury, Rommel shared precisely the same food and conditions as his men.

ABOVE Field Marshal Claude
Auchinleck, Wavell's suc-
cessor and a commander to
whose tactical skill Rommel
paid tribute in a letter
from El Alamein.

drilled his two Panzer divisions – the 15th and 21st – in training periods with other arms, perfecting the techniques of assault.

He decided to time his attack for the second half of November. Berlin told him to postpone it, but Rommel ignored this advice and went ahead with his plans. It was to be a costly decision, for the British had not been idle either. Rommel refused to listen to the warnings that he received that the British were planning an offensive which might occur before his own plans came to fruition. When the British did start their offensive, Rommel was taken by surprise; although his tactical acrobatics saved him from disaster, the overall outcome was a six-week retreat across all those precious miles of desert he had won the previous spring, so that by the end of the year he was almost back where he had started from, at El Agheila.

In these months he was to have his first experience of General Auchinleck's influence on the campaign – at times exercised no less decisively on the course of some of Rommel's battles than Rommel's own influence was. When Auchinleck had arrived in Cairo to succeed Wavell, he reached a fairly early conclusion that British forces could not return to the offensive in the western desert until the situations elsewhere in the theatre – in Cyprus and Syria – were made secure. Churchill was badgering him as usual, and Auchinleck initially agreed that Tobruk might not be defensible after September, particularly if Rommel advanced far enough east to take the airfield at Sidi Barrani, thus putting Tobruk out of the range of British fighter cover.

The offensive that Auchinleck was planning, which came to be called Crusader, was something he refused to be rushed into until the right preparations were made. As his biographer, John Connell, says, one of the characteristics of the desert war was that if you wanted anything, you brought it with you. So, in preparation for Crusader, Auchinleck organised the construction of large forward supply-dumps; the railway from Alexandria was extended farther westward; and a pipeline for fuel was laid along 150 miles. There is an inescapable contrast between these deliberate and methodical preparations for a British offensive and the impression which Rommel nearly always gives of an almost haphazard approach to the problem of supply. This may partly have been due to the fact that in the desert he was not in sole command of the supply organisation, and that there was constant feuding about it with the Italians – aggravated by the different equipment the two allies used. Nevertheless, one suspects of Rommel that he was always a little too ready to bewail the lack of supplies, and to imply that the supply organisation had let him down, without seeing that in desert war an acute awareness of supply was absolutely central to every tactical appreciation, and not just a piece of tangential and tiresome housekeeping which quartermasters must look after while the commander gets on with the serious business of fighting. He was haunted by the vision of turning into one of those generals 'of high intellectual powers who had been defeated by a less intelligent but stronger willed adversary' simply because they had listened to the advice of their quartermasters.

The best thing is for the commander himself to have a clear picture of the potentialities of his supply organisation and to base all his demands on his own estimate. This will force the supply staffs to develop their initiative, and though they may grumble, they will as a result produce many times what they would have done if left to themselves.

On 26 October, Rommel issued orders for his own attack, to start between 15 and 20 November. When his staff produced photo-reconnaissance pictures of the newly-built British railway as evidence of their offensive preparations, he refused to look at them and threw them down on the ground. He appeared to have become so obsessed with his own plans for the attack on Tobruk – perhaps he was nervous of letting this moment slip by him particularly when he was, in essence, going against the advice and instructions which he had received from the supreme command in Berlin – that he rejected all the very reliable intelligence available to him about the imminence of the British attack.

Meanwhile, Auchinleck and his new 8th Army commander, General Cunningham, were making their final dispositions. They agreed that the overall objective for General Cunningham should be the destruction of the enemy forces in the desert; this to be achieved by a feint towards Tobruk by a motorised infantry division in order to lure Rommel's two Panzer divisions out of the protected positions in the Bardia area, so that the 30th Corps with its armour could do battle with them in the open, unaided by the joint infantry and minefield defences which Rommel had built up with such skill; and finally to use the other corps, No. 13, to contain the bulk of Rommel's forces

Luftwaffe General Frölich, (right in both pictures) was a key member of Rommel's staff. Rommel incessantly demanded more air cover than Frölich could, or Hitler would, provide. In his diary Rommel wrote: 'The first and most serious danger was that which threatened us from the air'.

in their existing defences along the frontier line in the Bardia. Capuzzo and Sidi Omar areas.

The night before the start of the battle, 17 November, was tempestuous in more ways than one. It was cold, and there were bitter squalls of sleet and rain interspersed with flashes of lightning. About two hundred miles behind the German lines, a small party of British commandos under Colonel Keyes landed from the sea at Beda Littoria, and shot up an installation which they thought was Rommel's headquarters (as it had been some time previously), but which was now occupied by men from a quartermaster's unit, four of whom were killed. Rommel himself, unaware of the danger, was in Rome, probably at the opera with his wife, who had come to Italy for a short break to be with him on his fiftieth birthday.

When he got back to Africa the next day, the British attack was about to begin. The torrential rain had put all airfields out of operation, so that there was no air reconnaissance, and the British forces therefore achieved almost total surprise when they advanced to the first attack. Rommel was reluctant to believe that it was anything more than another reconnaissance in force and, for the best part of the first day's fighting, he refused to abandon his cherished plan to attack Tobruk and instead concentrate on the British threat.

The battle started with a British advance along three lines of attack, all leaving Rommel's main defences in Bardia and Sollum on their right, as they struck out across the desert from positions much farther south. The right-hand column, nearest Rommel's positions, soon came into contact with the 21st Panzer division, and was brought to a halt with fairly heavy losses. The centre column managed to push on right through to the Sidi Rezegh area, overlooking Tobruk. The third column came into contact with one of Rommel's Italian divisions, the Ariete, and its advance slowed down. General Norrie, commanding the 30th Corps from which all these prongs emerged, soon decided to transfer some of his armour from the left wing to help out on the right against the 21st Panzer, leaving the South African division to continue engaging the Ariete on its own. The result was that, by the second day of the battle, the formations of the 30th Corps were spread out across a swathe of desert about fifty miles long and about fifteen wide.

Rommel's staff sensed this dispersal the next day and were keen to compensate for their overall numerical inferiority by

'There was no air reconnaissance and the British achieved almost total surprise when they attacked'

concentrating all the German armour and picking off the lesser British elements of the 30th Corps, one by one. But this did not happen, partly because Rommel sent General Cruewell, the Africa Corps commander, off on a wild chase to destroy non-existent British armour in the Bardia area, and partly because, in this battle for the first time, formations under Rommel's command had become big enough to have staffs and commanders, such as Generals Cruewell and von Ravenstein, who had active independent minds of their own and who thus tended to operate with more initiative than Rommel's previous subordinates. This, in turn, made it harder for Rommel to impose his own distinctive control on the battle all the time.

By 21 November, after three days of fighting, the British were still consolidating their position round Sidi Rezegh, and hoping to link up with the 70th Division, which had been given orders to break out of Tobruk. General Cunningham had given this order on a misapprehension: he thought that the decisive tank battle which the British had been planning had already occurred, thus warranting a decision to move into the second phase involving the Tobruk breakout. In fact, it was not the decisive tank battle at all, but only a lesser encounter in the Sidi Omar area between some of Rommel's armour and the British 4th Armoured Brigade. It was broken off when Rommel pulled back the armour to the Sidi Rezegh area – not because he had been beaten, as Cunningham thought, but because he felt that the British in that area were getting dangerously close to a link-up with the forces in Tobruk.

It was in the Sidi Rezegh area that this period of the battle now became concentrated. Both German and Italian forces were deployed there to prevent the British link-up, and a situation developed in which each side was sandwiched between opposing forces. Looking eastward from Tobruk, for instance, the positions were: British, Italian, British, German, British, occupying an area of the desert measuring about sixty miles long and varying between five and forty miles deep. Each position involved troops facing threats and attacks from almost every direction, and the clash of armour which ensued lasted three days.

At the end of it, Rommel, Cruewell and von Ravenstein, often acting quite independently of each other and without contact, had had the best of almost every engagement, had recaptured the airfield at Sidi Rezegh and had virtually seen

The élan of German
motorised units was throughout, remarkable. Men and
vehicles seemed welded
together into fast and
dexterous fighting machines.
The British, by contrast,
were described by Rommel
as guilty of 'a rigid inability
to move quickly'.

WH-683309

the 7th Armoured Division off that particular field of battle. The British had withdrawn; but at least they were still in one piece, while the Germans suffered extensive losses which they could ill afford. The desert was littered with the charred hulks of literally hundreds of vehicles. The tank strength of both sides was now reduced to between seventy and eighty apiece.

While this slugging match was in progress, the British 13th Corps, led by the New Zealand Division, was continuing the advance towards Tobruk which Cunningham had ordered at the same time as he assented to the breakout by the 70th Division coming the other way. The New Zealanders' advance took them along the northern edge of the area in which there had been such fierce fighting. And it came as an unwelcome surprise to Rommel. He had successfully accounted for the first British thrust to Tobruk, but at considerable cost to his own units. Now he had a choice: to send all his forces to engage the advancing 13th Corps, risking then the possibility that the bruised but intact 30th Corps, and particularly the 7th Armoured Division, would regroup and link up with Tobruk behind him; to finish the job of destroying the 30th Corps' armour, thus risking the chance that the 13th Corps would manage in the time to join up with Tobruk; or to retreat with all his forces to Gazala as he had been advised to do by Hitler in the summer when he found himself in front of Tobruk with inadequate forces.

In the end, on 23 November, Rommel decided to choose none of these courses. Instead he decided to gather up his armour – or what was left of it – and, as he cabled that night to Berlin, to destroy the 7th Armoured Division, which lay slightly to the south and east of him on the way to the Egyptian frontier, and then to advance to Sidi Omar, on the frontier, to attack the enemy in the Sollum area, presumably with the intention of taking the advancing 13th Corps in the rear and linking up with his troops who were still holding out in the Bardia/Halfaya positions.

Just for a moment, the extraordinarily fast-moving but confusing and indistinct pattern of Crusader can be frozen long enough to catch both commanders in a single moment of decision, for, while Rommel was making this quite unexpected choice, a crisis of confidence was gripping the British leadership. General Cunningham had lost his nerve. Having lost so many tanks, he feared for the safety of his infantry divisions in the 13th Corps under the ravages of Rommel's Panzers. Should

'A crisis of confidence was gripping the British leadership'

RIGHT The vital desert railway, extended by the British, ran between Alexandria and Tobruk.

FAR RIGHT A German tank-trap, typical of the skilful defences which Rommel built up in the Bardia area.

BELOW British Cruiser tanks advance.

he continue the battle, at such risk possibly to the security of all Egypt? He decided that the magnitude of this decision was too much for him alone, and signalled for Auchinleck to come up from Cairo. Auchinleck, accompanied by the Air Commander-in-Chief, Air Marshal Tedder, flew up immediately. After Cunningham had briefed him, Auchinleck replied that he had no doubt whatever that their only course was to continue the offensive with every means at their disposal. At last, Rommel was being opposed by an equal will.

Auchinleck, in his official despatch, later explained his reasons, and in the process gave a not inaccurate analysis of Rommel's real situation at this moment in the battle. He also showed himself to be master of both strategic and tactical

Tobruk: an Allied gunner
in a battlefield strewn with
knocked-out vehicles.

New Zealanders recovering
a captured Allied tank from
its new German crew.

thinking in a way which Rommel himself, for all his flair and
natural instinct, never quite equalled.

It looked as if the enemy was hard pressed and stretched to the
limit [he wrote], and this was borne out by his behaviour at this
period of the battle: he was thrusting here, there and everywhere
in what seemed to me a desperate effort to throw us off our balance,
create chaos in our ranks, and so pave the way for regaining the
initiative. The enemy, it is true, had temporarily succeeded in
seizing the local tactical initiative, but the strategical initiative
remained with us: we were attacking, he was defending. This
general initiative it was at all costs essential to retain.

But how nearly Rommel, in his next trick, created just that
chaos and loss of balance which Auchinleck was at such pains
to prevent. Rommel's plan was not quite as he had described
it in his cable to Berlin. He was to put himself at the head of the
Africa Corps and drive round behind both the 30th Corps
(including the 7th Armoured Division), which was immediately
between him and the frontier, and also the 13th Corps whose
positions were on the frontier. He wanted then to force the
13th Corps back against the minefields, which he had laid in

122

the Halfaya and Sollum area. In doing so, he hoped to cut off the line of retreat and of supply of both British corps. But the exhilaration of battle must by then have overcome him, affecting the coolness of his judgment, for the task he set himself involved an initial drive of at least sixty miles of desert even before he reached the frontier wire, and he would have to go well past the wire before he could swing up to the left towards Sollum. Yet Rommel told his subordinates that he intended to complete the whole operation that day and be back possibly by that night. To von Ravenstein he said: 'You have a chance of ending this campaign tonight.'

On the morning of the 24th, Rommel put himself at the head of the column and waited impatiently for the Panzers to fuel up. Eventually, he could wait no more, and at 10.30 in the morning he set off at the head of just one Panzer regiment, with the rest of the corps following at noon. Rommel was destined to create almost as much chaos and confusion among his own staff and headquarters as he was in the headquarters of the 30th Corps, on which he bore down at the start of what has come to be known as his 'dash to the wire'.

The immediate effect on the British of this German armada, coming unexpectedly out of the battle area and heading straight for their rear echelons, was to induce a state of near panic. The confusion was indescribable as staff officers and supply units, more used to the ordered routines of a life comfortably to the rear of the battle, suddenly found themselves in a helter-skelter nine-hour rush back to the wire and beyond. Everyone was running, no one knew quite from what. Rommel was said to be upon them, but from where, how and in what strength no one could say, or stop for a moment to find out. The worst was suspected.

General Cunningham himself was caught up in this panic. He was visiting the headquarters of the 7th Armoured Division when the alert sounded, and he narrowly escaped capture, or a worse disaster, when his Blenheim aircraft was shelled on take-off. When he reached his own headquarters at Maddalena, also on the wire but far to the south, his confidence was probably not helped by receiving instructions from Auchinleck to continue fighting 'to the last tank'. But in the new situation created by Rommel's dash, Auchinleck, though by then back in Cairo, finally decided that Cunningham still lacked the will to assert his authority over the battle. Cunningham was dismissed and replaced by General Ritchie, a reliable but unimaginative member of Auchinleck's staff.

Rommel had reached the wire, and went on for another nineteen miles before he turned north to direct his Panzer divisions on to their targets – one to Halfaya, the other to Sidi Omar. Then, returning down the wire alone, his truck broke down. But one of those staggering strokes of luck then occurred which are such an essential element in the battles of all great generals, and with which Rommel was so handsomely endowed. As he stood with Gause at the wire, shivering in the November dusk, General Cruewell drove up in his Mammoth and took him in. But they were not yet clear of trouble, for they could not find a way back through the wire. Rommel, in a fury, dismissed the ADC from the driving seat and took the wheel himself. But he did no better. That night, the whole operation reached a new peak of farce, almost of fantasy. At the height of the battle, while divisions, tanks, trucks' and thousands of people were racing to and fro across the sand, who would have guessed that the flower of the Panzer Group Africa lay huddled all night in the Mammoth, totally lost, and in enemy-dominated territory? Even then, during the next day, Rommel spent most of his time behind the British lines trying to recapture some control of the battle, but without success. The Panzer attacks which he had organised had both miscarried, and he suddenly realised that the British forces against him were still much more numerous and more organised than he had suspected when he started his dash. Moreover, Auchinleck's own will, through Ritchie, was making itself felt on the battle.

Eventually, well to the rear, Rommel's own staff under Colonel Westphal had to intervene and give their own orders to the Panzer divisions without waiting for Rommel to reappear. These orders countermanded Rommel's own, and when he finally turned up again at his headquarters, he was for a moment black with rage. But having slept on it, he appeared the next morning to recognise that the fault was his. However, it was not until the night of 27 November, over four days after he had started, that he eventually re-established this contact with his own staff. The two Panzer divisions were also by then reunited in an area in which they could again concentrate on eliminating the serious threat to the German position which had been developed by the New Zealand Division's advance toward Tobruk.

Throughout these days, Ritchie remained optimistic,

'Rommel lay huddled all night in the Mammoth, totally lost, in enemy-dominated territory'

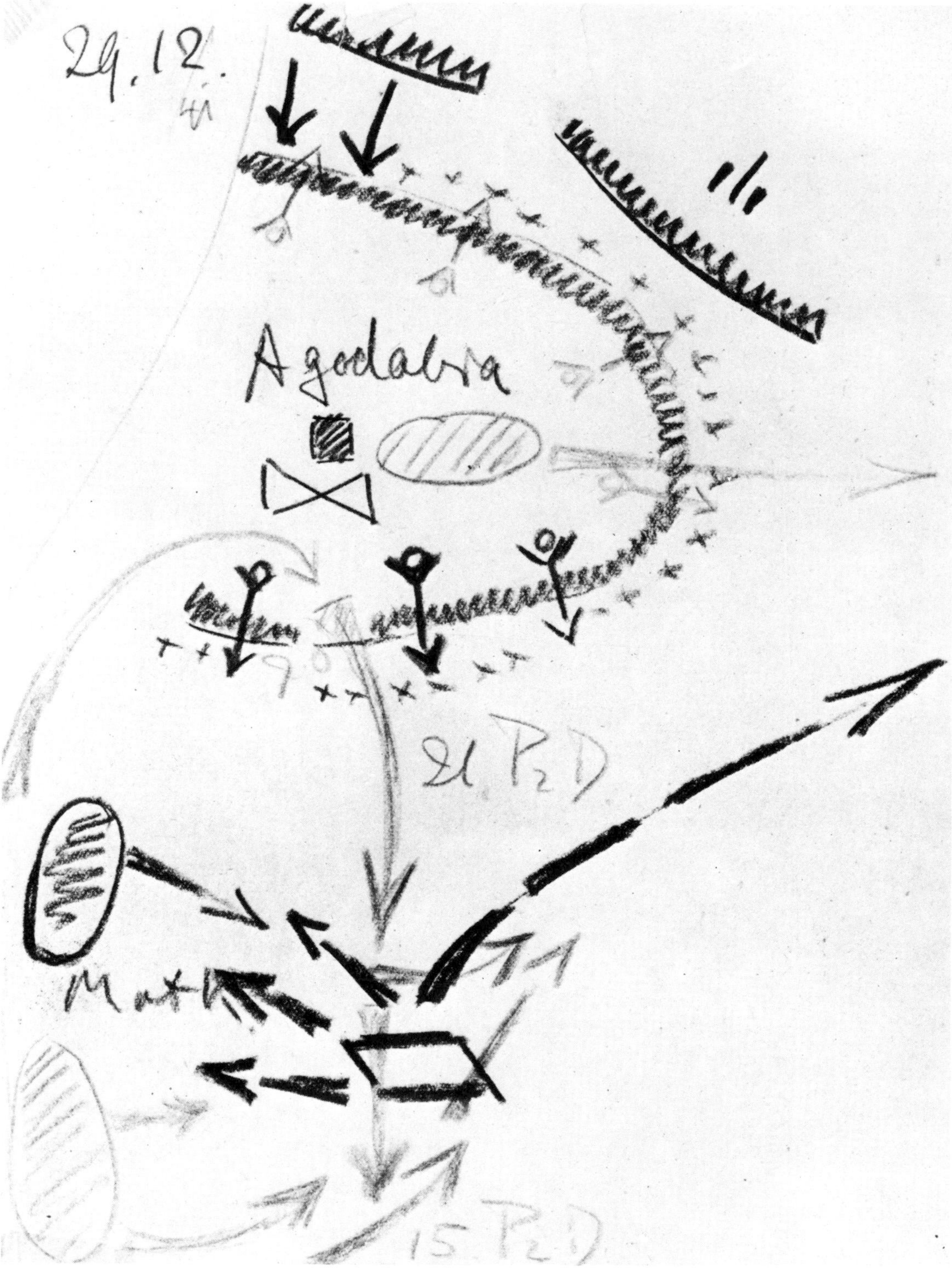

29.12.
41

Agedabia

21. P₂D

Mot

15. P₂D

ABOVE On the morning of 24 June Rommel made a bold dash ahead of his Panzers, right up to the 'wire', the Libyan–Egyptian border. This unexpected move created havoc amongst the Allied forces.

LEFT One of a series of sketches drawn by Rommel, plotting the stages of the battle round Agedabra.

127

and at one stage assumed that Rommel's general retreat westwards had already begun. In Cairo, Auchinleck told a member of his staff: 'We will get this stinker down where he belongs before long, I hope', and started to discuss plans for marching German prisoners through Cairo to convince the Egyptians of the British victory. But the 'stinker' was not down yet. Indeed, one of the features of the two weeks' fighting after Rommel came back from the wire is how very reluctant he was to accept that he had been defeated (which he had), and how he went on and on counter-attacking with a resilience which eventually even his own staff and troops could no longer sustain. His first objective was to reseal the ring round Tobruk, with the 13th Corps inside it. But, try as he might, he could not do it, though two New Zealand brigades were virtually destroyed in the course of this fighting between 28 and 30 November.

The Tobruk gap remained open, and Rommel's staff started to think in terms of a general retreat from Cyrenaica; but not Rommel. He seemed to be like a man possessed, but for once not with the kind of combative flair and the intuitive good judgment about the tactical situation which were usually such personal assets. Perhaps he just could not bring himself to admit that he had been defeated in a battle which he had refused to believe was going to take place. Anyway, he went on counter-attacking. On 3 December, after another demand for more supplies, he tried to send a relief operation forward to the forces which he had left behind in the Bardia, Halfaya and Sollum areas. The column was strafed and shelled mercilessly and the attack failed. Again, the next day, he tried another attack on the British positions east of Tobruk at El Duda, still without success. On 5 December, Auchinleck calculated that he would try to seize one last chance to throw the British off balance, and this duly came in an attack in the El Gubi area, from which Rommel eventually withdrew having made no headway and suffered heavy casualties. By this stage of the battle, the reports of the movement of divisions and brigades had really lost all meaning, but it is clear that most units had been reduced to about a tenth of their paper strength, sometimes more. Panzer divisions which one was accustomed to think of as a force of two hundred tanks were mustering no more than fifteen or twenty as a grand total. In fact, when the eventual losses were known, the Germans had lost 33,000 men killed or wounded, and 300 tanks, while the British had

A propaganda photograph issued by the German High Command in 1941, showing Africa Corps gunners manning a 3.7 cm Flak gun. In reality Rommel's forces were very poorly defended against air attack throughout the campaign.

Caught unawares, Allied
troops found themselves
fighting in a confused mêlée
of attack and
counter-attack.

suffered the loss of 17,000 killed or wounded and 278 tanks.

By 7 December, General Cruewell had come to the conclusion that the Africa Corps' losses were so severe that there must be a withdrawal. He pressed his case on Rommel, who eventually agreed to withdraw to a new line around Gazala. The Italians objected to this and were given fairly short shrift by Rommel. On 15 December, General Ritchie tried to get round Rommel's positions to the south and, though this attempt failed, Rommel decided that he could not hold the Gazala position; he prepared to retreat about 150 miles to Beda Fomm and Antelat, even though this meant abandoning his troops on the frontier, at which they eventually surrendered in January. On 24 December, Benghazi fell to the British, though not before Rommel had managed to take delivery of a welcome shipment of thirty tanks. These were put to good use in an engagement near El Haseiat on the 27th, when the 22nd Armoured Brigade was caught and surrounded by a much larger Panzer force. This battle was to represent the limit of the British pursuit.

So, by the end of the year, Rommel was back at Agedabia and the British had reconquered almost all of the Cyrenaica bulge. But, once again, the geometry of General Fuller's elastic was at work. The British were over-extended, and their maintenance and supply were suffering from the effects of the rapid advance after Crusader. The turn round, with Rommel chasing them back across Cyrenaica, was to be as sudden, and then as complete, as their own advance had been since 18 November.

Rommel's dash to the wire has remained the subject of keen but unresolved military controversy. Liddell Hart's conclusion is that he was right to try the deep counter-thrust, as the one move that offered a good chance of tilting the scales decisively in his favour. On the other hand, it is easy, since the operation failed, to believe that he was wrong to do it. Certainly, it was a stroke of quite unprecedented imagination and élan. Perhaps in the end it comes down to will – that much-ignored but eventually dominant element in every battle. For one of the first times in his fighting life, Rommel found, in Auchinleck, an opposing commander whose will was as great as, if not greater than, his own, and whose willpower was at that moment reinforced by a clarity of thought and the resources to underwrite it, which on Rommel's side were not to be found at that time.

131

6 Advance
to El Alamein

THE START OF 1942 saw Rommel's army facing British forces on the Tripolitania-Cyrenaica border more or less where they had both been nearly a year before. In the course of the next twelve months, however, Rommel was to advance nearly six hundred miles eastwards – in two bounds of about three hundred miles each – reach the end of his logistical 'elastic' and then come hurtling back the whole way, and beyond.

Considering that he was still suffering the consequences of his defeat in Crusader until the middle of January 1942 – the surrender of Axis troops at Halfaya, Bardia and Sollum occurred on 2, 11 and 17 January respectively – Rommel's resilience in springing back into the attack is really remarkable. As early as 5 January, the arrival in Tripoli of a convoy with fifty-five new tanks and twenty armoured cars encouraged him to start making new offensive plans. In Cairo, the day before this, Auchinleck was telling Ritchie that he did not think that a counter-attack by Rommel was likely, but it would be typical of him to do it and, if he tried, he would make sure that his force was properly equipped.

Typical indeed! A week later Colonel Westphal came back from an air reconnaissance over the British positions and told Rommel that they were ripe for a surprise German counter-attack. Serious planning started, and Rommel gave his final orders on 19 January. He told his divisional commanders then, but took care to let neither the Italian nor German High Commands into the secret, so that he would suffer less interference. On the day on which Rommel's final orders were given, Auchinleck and Ritchie were making their own plans for the immediate future. Ritchie told his Commander-in-Chief that the state of repair and maintenance of his mechanised units ruled out an offensive until mid-February. Auchinleck believed that he would then be strong enough either to force Rommel out of El Agheila or to surround him. It was clear that Ritchie could not for long stay in his present position in the Cyrenaica bulge, which was not tenable. He should either advance west of Agheila or else retire. Auchinleck asked him therefore to advance farther into Tripolitania – to Tripoli if he could. But he added a prophetic rider to these orders – presumably on the basis of his understanding of how extremely tenuous was Ritchie's position unless he could continue the advance. Should a withdrawal from Cyrenaica become necessary, he wrote, Ritchie should take

PREVIOUS PAGES Rommel and his staff inspecting a knocked-out Allied tank. The seasoned German Panzers made short work of some of the inexperienced Allied relief troops.

134

British troops in an Italian
P.O.W. camp near Benghazi
after the recapture of the
town by the Germans,
February 1942.

the southern route back to the frontier wire, and then to
Mersah Matruh. Two further paragraphs stated that, in those
circumstances, Auchinleck would not hold permanently
either Tobruk or any other locality west of the wire, and that
work on the El Alamein defensive position should now be
speeded up.

Two days later, on 21 January, in Auchinleck's own words,
'The improbable occurred and Rommel attacked.' The British
troops facing him belonged to the newly-arrived 1st Armoured
Division which had been sent up to relieve the 7th Armoured
Division so that it could recover from the ravages of Crusader.
The division was inexperienced in the desert, and also contained three cavalry regiments which had only comparatively
recently converted from horses to armour. They were a poor
match for the seasoned armoured warriors in the Panzer divisions, mounted as they were on newer and stronger tanks. In

the first four days of the fighting, both sides made misjudgments – Rommel thought that he had the British division surrounded and in the bag, while the British were unaware of the strength and purpose of his attack and still thought that it must be no more than a reconnaissance in force. However, in the space of a few days, the 15th Panzer Division had already got through to Msus; Benghazi was to fall shortly afterwards and the whole British position in the bulge of western Cyrenaica became untenable. On 30 January, a gloomy Auchinleck concluded that the British forces were at the time not capable of meeting Rommel in the open unless they had a majority of at least a two to one.

Ten days later, Auchinleck sent Ritchie revised instructions. These were first, to hold the enemy as far west of Tobruk as possible (this turned out to be the Gazala line); secondly, to organise a force to recapture what he had lost as soon as possible; thirdly, to try to regain the landing grounds in the Derna Mechili area and deny them to the enemy; and fourth, to avoid being invested in Tobruk if he had to retreat farther back to well-prepared positions in the Sollum area. So Ritchie settled down to consolidate his forces near Gazala, and prepare the 8th Army for the next big battle which was not to occur until May.

'Mussolini criticised his own generals for not riding [like Rommel] at the head of their tank columns'

Meanwhile, Rommel was exultant. On 4 February, he wrote to Lu: 'We have got Cyrenaica back. It went like greased lightning. I hope to be home in ten days' time for a bit of leave.' However, he had not taken account of the Italians, and was not to be home for some time. Ciano, the Italian Foreign Minister, was noting in Rome that Mussolini was extolling Rommel, and criticising his own generals for not riding, like the German, at the head of their tank columns. According to Ciano, the Bersaglieri were enthusiastic about Rommel, had given him their feathers and carried him in triumph on their shoulders shouting that they were sure that with him they could reach Alexandria. Neither the attitude of Mussolini – however volatile it was – nor that of the Bersaglieri was likely to endear Rommel to the Italian generals with whom he had to work. On 10 February, he wrote to Lu: 'Trouble with Rome who don't agree with the way I'm running things and would be best pleased to see us get out of Cyrenaica.' The Italians took back an army corps because 'I'm not sitting as far back as they would like me to. They'll be sorry for it.' In spite of his desire to push on as fast as he could, he had to settle down in virtually defensive positions opposite the British, who were similarly deployed. They both then prepared for the May offensive.

For the next few months, the importance of the desert campaign was very much subordinated to wider strategic issues. The fall of Singapore on 15 February, and the retreat from Burma, made it appear likely that Middle East Command would have to send more troops to help out in Asia. On the German side, the preparations for the second summer offensive in Russia became particularly preoccupying in view of the setback which the Germans had received that winter at the very gates of Moscow. But, along with these wider questions, there was one issue on which both sides seemed to agree – Malta.

The situation of Malta was intimately linked with the North African fortunes of both the British and the Axis forces. It dominated Rommel's supply lines and was also highly relevant to the occasional British convoy which braved the Mediterranean run to Alexandria rather than the very much longer route round the Cape. In early 1942, the island was subjected to ever-increasing attacks by the Luftwaffe, to the point at which it was thought in London that Auchinleck must start a new offensive in the desert to relieve the pressure on Malta. Rommel and his masters were also discussing Malta. The German arguments swung round the question whether Rommel's plans for a major offensive eastwards could ever be really viable so long as a hostile Malta lay athwart his rear. Should not the destruction of the Malta base therefore take precedence over Rommel's plans for a further advance eastwards in the desert? The outcome of a conference held by Hitler in late April was that Rommel would be allowed to attack as far as Tobruk, provided that once Tobruk was taken he would then go over to the defensive, while the Axis powers concentrated on eliminating the threat from Malta. Rommel objected to this as short-sighted, though the failure to adhere to this plan after the fall of Tobruk was probably one of the main reasons for his subsequent undoing.

So both sides continued throughout the early spring to work out plans for an offensive at Gazala. The result was bound to be that somebody would get in first. This time it was to be Rommel. In fact, the way in which the British had prepared their positions at Gazala rather belied the talk of an offensive which had eventually been agreed between London and

137

Cairo. The position was based much more on a defensive rather than an offensive strategy, and made sense only if the other side attacked first. To that extent, Rommel obliged.

Ritchie had constructed something that was rare in the desert – a fully-developed position of defence in depth. It stirred Rommel to point out that desert conditions were such that any rigid system of defence is bound to lead to disaster. Only a mobile defence is likely to be successful, he said. He recognised that individual fortified positions were useful to prevent the enemy from undertaking operations in a particular direction, but that the manning of the positions should not be at the expense of mobile defence. In fact, in the Gazala battle which was shortly to start, the British intended to combine fixed points of defence with a mobile armoured element, just as Rommel postulated, but the battle developed in such a way that they eventually suffered from the disadvantages of what amounted to a fixed defence.

General Ritchie had constructed a line south of Gazala which consisted of a whole series of fortified 'boxes', heavily wired and mined, in which he put his infantry. The boxes were linked by an enormous screen of minefields. In the rear, and slightly to the south, he held his armour in reserve. It was a pattern reminiscent of the infantry squares at Waterloo, with the cavalry kept intact behind. The southern edge of this line was a fort at Bir Hacheim, which was manned by a brigade of the Free French. Auchinleck, in his pre-battle appreciation, believed that Rommel would either swirl round Bir Hacheim and drive straight towards Tobruk, cutting into the rear of the British position, or else feint at Bir Hacheim and then direct the main weight of his assault in a frontal attack on the centre of the line of boxes, hoping to break through to Tobruk from there. Auchinleck thought that the latter plan was the most likely, and also the most dangerous as it would cut the British line in two; but if Rommel swept round the south of Bir Hacheim and then advanced north towards the coast he should present a favourable target to the British armour, and suffer from a long, exposed, dog-leg line of communication to his rear.

None the less, on the other side of the line, Rommel was deciding on the bolder course round Bir Hacheim, leaving his Italian divisions to feint forward at the northern and central parts of the British line. He ordered the Ariete division to attack Bir Hacheim, while the two Panzer divisions and the

'*In the Gazala battle the British intended to combine fixed points of defence with a mobile armoured element, just as Rommel postulated*'

138

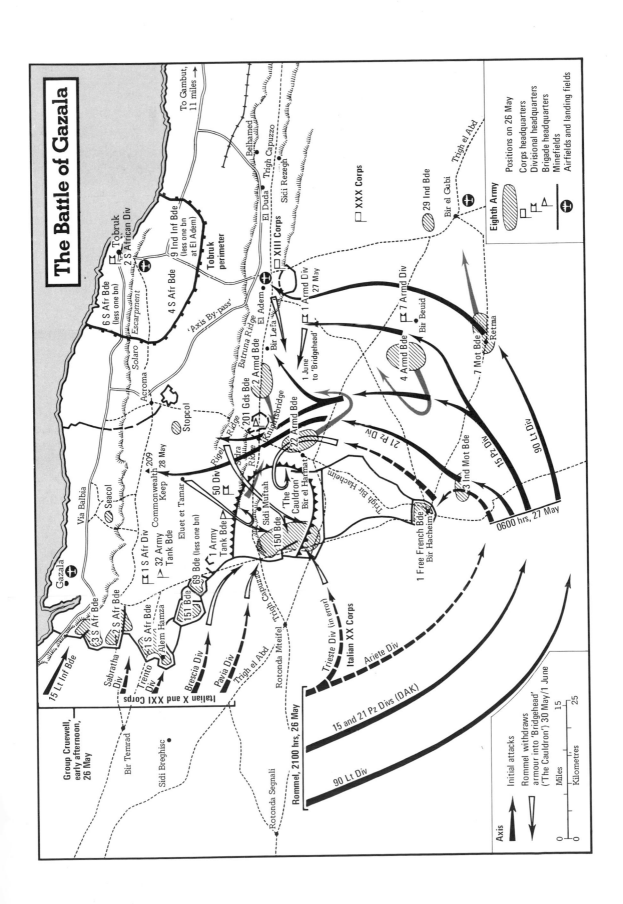

The Battle of Gazala

To Gambut, 11 miles →

Belhamed

Tobruk
2 S African Div
6 S Afr Bde (less one bn)
4 S Afr Bde
9 Ind Inf Bde (less one bn at El Adem)
Tobruk perimeter

Trigh Capuzzo
Sidi Rezegh
El Duda
'Axis By-pass'
Solaro Escarpment
Acroma

Batruna Ridge
El Adem
Bir Lefa
1 Armd Div 27 May
XIII Corps

Bir Beuid
7 Armd Div
4 Armd Bde
1 June to 'Bridgehead'
2 Armd Bde

Trigh el Abd
29 Ind Bde
Bir el Gubi

Knightsbridge
201 Gds Bde
22 Armd Bde
21 Pz Div
7 Mot Bde
Retma

Eighth Army
Positions on 26 May
Corps headquarters
Divisional headquarters
Brigade headquarters
Minefields
Airfields and landing fields

XXX Corps

Rigel Ridge
Sidra Ridge
Commonwealth Keep 28 May
209
Stopcol
3 Ind Mot Bde
15 Pz Div
90 Lt Div

Via Balbia
Seacol
Gazala

Eluet et Tamar
50 Div
Sidi Muftah
150 Bde
'The Cauldron'
Bir el Harmat
Trigh Bir Hacheim
0600 hrs, 27 May

1 S Afr Div
32 Army Tank Bde
69 Bde (less one bn)
1 Army Tank Bde
1 Free French Bde
Bir Hacheim

3 S Afr Bde
2 S Afr Bde
1 S Afr Bde
Alem Hamza
151 Bde
Sabratha Div
Trento Div
Brescia Div
Pavia Div
Trigh el Abd
Trigh Capuzzo
Rotonda Mteifel
15 Lt Inf Bde

Italian X and XXI Corps

Bir Temrad
Sidi Breghisc

Group Cruewell, early afternoon, 26 May

Trieste Div (in error)
Italian XX Corps
Ariete Div

Rotonda Segnali

Rommel, 2100 hrs, 26 May

15 and 21 Pz Divs (DAK)

90 Lt Div

Axis
Initial attacks
Rommel withdraws armour into 'Bridgehead' ('The Cauldron') 30 May/1 June

0   15   25
Miles
0   15   25
Kilometres

ABOVE Barbed-wire defences
around a bunker position.

RIGHT German soldier
removing a mine.

90th Light Division would advance north-east from the Bir Hacheim hinge, and engage and destroy the British armour which he expected was between there and El Adem, his first night's objective. He then hoped to seize Sidi Rezegh, farther east, before turning back to the west and attacking the British positions in the Gazala line from both sides – his armour in their rear, the Italian infantry divisions in their front. Tobruk he intended to leave for the subsequent two days. Rommel's plans and supplies for the whole battle were based on a calculation that it would last only four days. This was absurdly optimistic – indeed, almost ruinously so. In the event, Rommel found himself fighting almost continuously for six weeks, with the result that when his advance was finally brought to a halt at the first battle of El Alamein in early July, he had hardly a tank to his name, troops in a state of utter exhaustion and a disastrous paucity of supplies.

Rommel's attack was launched on the night of 26 May, with all his armour sweeping down towards the Bir Hacheim hinge. British armoured car patrols spotted the advance and reported it back, but, for all that, the 7th Armoured Division was surprised and caught unprepared when Rommel's armour rounded Bir Hacheim and struck into its positions early the next morning. In those first actions, however, the Panzers received a nasty shock from the newly-arrived Grant tanks, which were definitely superior to the Panzers'. They also discovered that the new six-pounder gun was helping to restore the previous British inferiority in anti-tank guns.

By the end of the first day, Rommel's position was distinctly unfavourable. He confessed that the principal cause of his failure either to disrupt the British mobile forces, or to advance to the coast to cut off the British position, lay in an underestimate of the strength of the British armoured divisions and the effect of the new Grant tank which 'had torn great holes in our ranks'. Had Auchinleck's original advice to the 8th Army been heeded – to hold back the armour and then concentrate it in a counter-attack against Rommel's weakened position – the German commander would have been in serious trouble. The British armour would have been well placed to force Rommel back against the British boxes and the minefields round them, cut off from his supplies and reinforcements. As it was, the British armoured units were eventually sent in one by one to attack the Africa Corps, thus eroding the overall British superiority until it was non-existent.

The course of the battle during these first few days was so fierce, however, that it took some time for Rommel to see a clear advantage emerging. His supply situation round Bir Hacheim was always critical, with British forces causing havoc among the convoys of soft-skinned vehicles bringing vital fuel and ammunition to his Panzers. They had to come round because they could not get through the screen of minefields. Rommel himself went back once and personally led a supply column to the Africa Corps. Naturally, he was always in the thick of the fighting, his status as army group commander having in no way reduced either his lust for battle, or his capacity to get to the very centre of the storm. He came under fire from all and sundry – British, Italian and even German guns, when he was bombed and strafed by his own Stukas (or rather Kesselring's) while unloading ammunition after a sortie. His position behind the boxes became so critical that he urged the Italian divisions to attack the British line to make certain that no other British units would be relieved from the front line and turned in on the 'cauldron' in the middle, where Rommel and his Panzers were taking on all-comers from almost all directions.

At this stage, the British Command was still optimistic of success. Auchinleck instructed Ritchie to press on with the battle by mounting an attack along the coast to the north, the very thing which Rommel hoped would happen when he gave the Italian divisions their orders. Ritchie, however, demurred, believing that the cauldron should be mopped up first. So a counter-offensive called 'Aberdeen' was arranged, and on 5 June, both the corps of the 8th Army sent in attacks designed to dislodge Rommel from his central position behind the boxes. However, in the words of Michael Carver in *Tobruk*, when the attack went in, it was like 'sticking one's arm into a wasp's nest', and it failed to dislodge Rommel.

One of the most marked impressions of British conduct during this and other desert battles is of the interminable conferences and the exchange of series after series of long, well-argued memoranda. By contrast, Rommel was not interested in such verbalisation – certainly not once a battle had started. Nor is this contrast merely the result of the different styles of literature from the two sides. It was, in fact, a constant German criticism of Rommel that during his battles he abandoned all kinds of routine. Kesselring visited the Gazala battle shortly after General Cruewell was captured, and had to take

'He was always in the thick of the fighting . . . he came under fire from British, Italian and even German guns, when he was bombed by his own Stukas'

Field Marshal Kesselring (centre) was yet another of the critics of Rommel's inspired, but erratic, command.

over temporary command of the Africa Corps. He complained that he found it difficult since 'Rommel issues no orders, cannot be reached. Moreover the stimulating effect of Rommel's presence on the decisive flank was off-set by his immediate exposure to all the fluctuations of the battle.' Even if these strictures were right in principle, in this particular case they were wrong. Rommel's position on what Kesselring described as the decisive flank was in fact the nodal point of the battle, and was probably crucial to its successful outcome. From there, he dominated the fighting and was also, in the end, able to gauge how important that position was, something that he might not have been able to do from a more remote head-

German army engineers
bridging an anti-tank trench
on the outskirts of
Tobruk, July 1942.

144

quarters. It was as though the Africa Corps had its hands gripping the British throat. It was not yet strong enough to overcome the whole body, but was squeezing harder and harder all the time. And the 8th Army could not shake it off.

The British brigades in their boxes were gradually surrounded and overrun by Rommel. The rest of the 8th Army lay scattered over the desert. Ritchie, at this time, believed that the Axis forces had suffered equally. It is true that they had suffered materially, but positionally there was no question that Rommel had the decisive advantage. After he had destroyed a number of the most important boxes in the centre of the British line, he turned with all his might on Bir Hacheim, where the Free French had been gallantly resisting the assault of two Axis divisions for over a week. It eventually fell to Rommel on 10 June. He then, without delay, ordered his forces north for the final decisions round El Adem. That, and a number of other suspicions, brought a worried Auchinleck up from Cairo to 8th Army headquarters. He says that he found the atmosphere there good, and morale high, and so returned semi-reassured to Cairo.

The fighting on 12 June ended with Rommel in command of the ridge which overlooked Tobruk's defences. What remained of the British mobile forces were sheltering in the two boxes at El Adem and Knightsbridge, or strung out precariously along the fifteen-mile salient between them. On the night of the 13th, the guards brigade evacuated Knightsbridge, and Ritchie started to consider withdrawing what was left of his infantry in the Gazala line before they were completely cut off. But Auchinleck told him that he must stay where he was. A rasping endorsement of this came from the pen of Churchill in London: 'Retreat would be fatal', he said. 'This is a business not only of armour but of willpower. God bless you all.'

But the British position was sliding all the time. While Auchinleck was assuring Churchill that he had no intention of allowing Tobruk to be besieged, or of giving it up, Ritchie was working at cross purposes and pursuing a course of action which was bound to make nonsense of Auchinleck's undertakings. By 17 June, El Adem was lost; the Africa Corps had cut the coast road east of Tobruk, and was turning back west to roll up the British forces. With the loss of El Adem, Tobruk this time was virtually in Rommel's hands, though as late as 19 June, Auchinleck was still protesting to General Smuts –

who had enquired after the fate of the South African Division in the Tobruk garrison – that he had no intention of giving it up. The correspondence between Auchinleck and Ritchie at this time shows Auchinleck becoming increasingly perturbed at the deliberate nature of the latter's preparations and the lack of urgency with which he seemed to be viewing the battle. 'Crisis may arise in a matter of hours not days', he said. He was right. But it was already too late: by the time that his messages arrived at Ritchie's headquarters on 21 June, Tobruk had fallen.

The capture of Tobruk was the high moment of Rommel's career. Hitler that day made him a Field Marshal. He was only fifty. In the last four years, he had come up fast. The promotion caused Mussolini pain, not because Rommel was out of favour – on the contrary the Duce shared in the general exultation and was boasting that in fifteen days they would establish a commissariat in Alexandria – but because it would mean having to promote the Italian generals to Field Marshal rank too. This can hardly have been to his liking, since he told Ciano that the Italian generals were the only thing which could stop Rommel reaching the Nile Delta!

ABOVE Tobruk has fallen, and Rommel, photographed outside his spartan field quarters, is a Field Marshal at fifty.

LEFT German troops in Tobruk's main square. The wall of the barber's shop still bears the improvised title 'Sweeney Todd, Tobruk.'

It is possible that Rommel also experienced a minor disappointment at Tobruk when he discovered the supplies which the British had left. John Connel reports in *Auchinleck* that, when Rommel met the South African Divisional Commander, General Koppler, and his staff after they had surrendered, he was so angry about this that he 'shouted and blustered at them like a sergeant major'. On the other hand, Rommel told a very different story that very day to Kesselring, who arrived to discuss whether they should continue the drive towards Egypt or now go over to the defensive, as had been previously agreed, and concentrate on the elimination of Malta. Kesselring was all for 'Operation Hercules' – the Malta plan, but Rommel insisted that he must go on and claimed that, with the capture of all the equipment at Tobruk, he could now do so. When Kesselring in his turn insisted, Rommel appealed directly over his head to Hitler and Mussolini, making a very early use of his right of direct access as a Field Marshal. Hitler and the Duce let him have his way. 'It is only once in a lifetime that the goddess of victory smiles', said the Führer. Cavallero, the Italian Chief-of-Staff, was instructed to fly out to Rommel on 26 June to work out the new directives.

147

Vital Allied supplies captured
in Tobruk.

In a moment of perhaps understandable but rash, ridiculous overconfidence, Rommel told him: 'I count on being in occupation of Cairo and Alexandria by 30 June' – four days.

Until the day before that, with the help of a little luck and a little more logic, Rommel might have been able to prove himself right. But on 25 June, Auchinleck finally left Cairo to come up and take over command of the 8th Army from General Ritchie. In the plane on the way up, he decided to make his real stand at El Alamein, not at the Mersah Matruh base into which Ritchie was even then retreating. This was just as well, since the British only just managed to break out of Mersah Matruh before Rommel surrounded them.

With the capture of Mersah Matruh and another huge amount of supplies, Rommel believed that the last fortress port in the desert was now his. However, there could be no rest for his nearly exhausted troops. Although he had captured a great deal of equipment and thousands of prisoners, the great bulk of the British infantry had managed to elude him and get back to the position at El Alamein, where the desert narrowed to about thirty miles between the sea and the

The chase to El Alamein: Rommel's exhausted troops begin the dusty trail towards defeat.

impassable Qattara depression. It was therefore doubly important for Rommel to get to El Alamein and overrun it before the 8th Army had time to organise itself and complete the defences. In fact, he was already too late. But nobody who witnessed the chaos on the British side would at that time have dared believe so. The few desert roads were crammed and blocked with retreating vehicles in convoys of a hundred miles and more. The days and nights were shattered by the thump of huge explosions as dump after dump which had been supplied with such sweat was blown up in the face of the advancing Germans. In Alexandria, the British fleet put to sea as a precaution. In the Delta, troops prepared to fight a last-ditch defence in a thousand ditches – the maze of irrigation canals. The scene which Auchinleck left behind' him in Cairo was pandemonium. The city was under curfew. Eastbound trains for Palestine were packed with refugees. Even members of the general staff at headquarters were evacuated if it was thought that they knew too much to risk capture. Auchinleck, at the front, was clearly not affected. 'I've never been a good loser. I'm going to win,' he said, and sent a message to all ranks in the

8th Army saying: 'The enemy hopes to take Egypt by bluff. Show him where he gets off.'

So both armies came to El Alamein. The battle of that name which most people now remember is that which was fought the following October, when General Montgomery succeeded in breaking through Rommel's defensive positions and sending him off on the long retreat back to Tunis. It was the start of the campaign which led to the strategic victory in North Africa. But the first battle of Alamein, fought in July between Rommel and Auchinleck, is of almost more decisive significance. It ended the possibility of a British strategic defeat in North Africa. After it, Rommel's eventual defeat was just a matter of time and resources. Between the two battles, the tide in North Africa turned.

Rommel intended to overrun the El Alamein position in much the same way as he had tackled previous British defences in the desert – either by going round their flanks or by piercing the centre and then swivelling round to cut off the rear. In view of the narrowness of the El Alamein gap, he could not go round the position, so he planned to pierce the centre of the British defences and fan out on either side behind them to cut off their retreat. For the first three days of the battle, he had the initiative, attacking here and there, hoping to implement his plan. After 4 July, the initiative hung in the balance, with a series of British counter-attacks designed to turn Rommel's own flank and drive him off. These were no more successful than Rommel's own earlier attempts. Then, for the next three weeks, both sides attacked and counter-attacked with ever-decreasing effect, like two boxers in the closing rounds of a fifteen-round match, whose punches are slower and weaker and, though they land in the target area, effect little decisive damage to the opponent. By the end of July, after one final British attempt to break through Rommel's front, the battle subsided in a situation of stalemate. It may have been a tactical stalemate, but it was a strategic defeat. Rommel was to advance no more.

Rommel's failure at the first battle of El Alamein can be ascribed to many factors. His first plan of attack failed because of inadequate reconnaissance, which meant that when the Germans pierced the first part of the British positions, and prepared to fan out, they found that the British defences were much deeper than expected, and were pinned down before they could make their outflanking manœuvre. By this time

'For three weeks both sides attacked and counter-attacked with ever-decreasing effect'

Rommel's divisions were each down to a strength of about twelve hundred fighting men and fifteen tanks, and Rommel himself was clearly nearing exhaustion. His letters to Lu adopt an increasingly weary, sometimes almost plaintive air; his exaggerations of the strength of the enemy become more marked; his attributions of the causes of defeat to the lack of supplies start to become more bitter. 'I'm rather tired and fagged out . . . the air is electric with crisis . . . my expectations bitterly disappointed.' He was by then probably already affected by a liver complaint which in the next battle, at the end of August, so incapacitated him that he could not get out of his truck. Yet, at one moment, he is telling Lu that he is physically well, and wearing shorts for the first time, before sinking quickly back into the gloom as the battle continues to go against him. 'Things are going downright badly for me . . .', he wrote, and 'it's enough to make one weep', in response to Auchinleck's technique of concentrating his attacks on the Italian units – the weakest parts of Rommel's line – forcing him to switch his already-exhausted German units backwards and forwards as emergency reinforcements. He tells Lu that it is the most difficult period he has ever been through, and later that he is tired and limp and that everyone is suffering from diarrhoea. This was not a picture of confidence, perhaps because in Rommel's mind it was already becoming clear that this was not just an ordinary setback which could be recouped by his normally inventive generalship. He was at the end of his tether, so were his troops, so were his supplies. There was nothing left with which to be inventive, and not much sign that the long-term prospect would change.

Against him, Auchinleck had the great psychological advantage of freshness. Despite the fact that he had been wrestling with momentous affairs of state in Cairo, his arrival to take over the 8th Army in the field must have had an extremely tonic effect on this essentially fighting soldier. Unlike the rest of the 8th Army, he was literally moving forward from Cairo, bringing with him a capacity for fresh thinking and confident application uncluttered by the sense of personal disaster and demoralisation which the recent defeats and retreat must have instilled in most of his troops. Rommel noticed this soon enough when he commented respectfully on Auchinleck's cool direction of the battle.

7 The Long Retreat

MORE THAN THIRTY YEARS after the event, the strategic significance of the first battle of El Alamein – the fact that it spelled the ultimate end of Rommel's position in North Africa – becomes much clearer than it was to the British at the time. Rommel, it is true, seems to have become increasingly infected with an almost unshakeable pessimism after it, only occasionally relieved by those frenzied bouts of activity which he found irresistible in the heat of battle. Moreover, he recognised that unless he could keep up the momentum of his advance from Gazala, and keep the British on the run so that they could not take advantage of their much shorter supply lines and much larger supplies, victory would in the end elude him.

The British leadership, on the other hand, clearly failed to appreciate the measure of Auchinleck's achievement. Churchill and his advisers descended *en masse* on Cairo in early August. During the Cairo meeting, Churchill was discovered stumping round his hotel bedroom fulminating: 'Rommel! Rommel! Rommel! Rommel! What else matters but beating him?' By the end of it, Churchill had decided to dismiss Auchinleck and and replace him with General Alexander, appointing General Montgomery to the command of the 8th Army. So, for the second time in his desert career, Rommel had the scalp of a British Commander-in-Chief to his credit. If victory had in fact eluded him already at El Alamein, he had none the less achieved a psychological victory by demoralising Churchill sufficiently to destroy his confidence in Auchinleck and blind him to what the latter had achieved. With Montgomery and Alexander against him, however, Rommel was to be less lucky – not only because of the personalities of those two generals, but because the political context of the desert battle had also changed.

In the autumn of 1942, Churchill politically needed a victory more than he had ever done – so much so, in fact, that he showed himself prepared to wait for it in a way in which he never had with Auchinleck and Wavell: 1942 had been a bad year for British arms; Churchill himself had had to fight a vote of censure in the Commons, and his position as Prime Minister had therefore been questioned. But the second half of 1942 also saw the development of a joint Anglo-American strategy which, when implemented, would naturally eclipse any independent operations which the British were likely to carry out. Planning for the Anglo-American landing in north-west

156

Africa – code-named Torch – was already in an advanced stage. It was thus doubly important for Churchill, on political grounds, to show that Britain could achieve a decisive victory of her own against the Axis forces before the centre of gravity of the alliance shifted to Washington and the opportunity for major independent initiatives passed away from Churchill and his war Cabinet.

At the time of the Cairo meeting, however, it was not America's entry into the war which dominated the discussion, but the question whether Russia was going to be able to resist Hitler's second offensive which was even then penetrating down into the Caucasus. In the light of that, it was important to Britain to prevent the Africa Corps from breaking through east of Suez and advancing to link up with the German Caucasian front somewhere in Asia Minor.

Rommel dashes to the front at El Alamein in characteristically bold and reckless fashion.

Rommel in an informal
meeting with Mussolini:
Il Duce added his own voice
to the clamour for victory
which pursued Rommel. He
liked nothing better than a
glamorous victory parade.

OPPOSITE When General
Montgomery, popular hero
of the El Alamein victory,
took over the 8th Army,
Rommel no doubt saw him
as merely the latest British
General to be 'tried out' in
North Africa, the successor
to a considerable line of
deposed commanders.

Rommel, too, was to become obsessed by the entry of
America into the war, to the point at which he became so convinced that the Axis was bound to lose that his strategic, overall pessimism must have affected his tactical judgment. But
during the summer of 1942, before this pessimism set in, and
before he was brought to a halt at El Alamein, he had been
thinking along the same lines as were the British in Cairo. He
sent a paper to Berlin which urged his command to consider
greater co-ordination between the Africa Corps and the
Russian offensive, by reinforcing the Africa Corps so that it
could thrust across Suez into Persia and Iraq, and thus cut off
the Russians' southern route for American supplies which
came through the port of Basra. He said later that his plan was
'turned down by people of limited vision as a complete fantasy',
and added, in justification, that 'anyone who fights a whole
world must think in continents'.

But by August 1942, his more immediate worry was how to
defeat the 8th Army and reach Suez before the weight of

British reinforcements built up to overwhelm him. Even before the first battle of El Alamein, he recognised the threat of the new quality and quantity of equipment which was arriving on the British side, and which, if continued unchecked, 'would clearly mean the end of us'. It made him doubly determined to keep up the pressure, rather than pause for his own shattered supply line to be reconditioned. When his first attack failed, 'our chance of overrunning the remainder of the 8th Army and occupying eastern Egypt at one stroke was irretrievably gone'.

However, for Rommel, at the time, there seemed to be no question of withdrawal. He clearly still believed that his own tactical weakness was better overcome by pressing on, in the hope of unbalancing the superior enemy; but more important, he had by his own optimism and boasting created such expectations in the minds of Hitler and Mussolini that he would almost certainly have lost his job if, only two weeks after predicting the capture of Cairo, and scarcely a month after talking about an advance into Persia and Iraq, he had to confess that he had no alternative but retreat. Mussolini, after all, had already ordered his white horse for the triumphal entry into Cairo, and had even had his finery flown out to an advanced position in Libya to enable him to make a quick return to Africa for the expected victory parade. The German and Italian High Commands had agreed that Egypt would be in the Italian sphere of influence, governed by an Italian civilian delegate with Rommel as Commander-in-Chief. Rommel had encouraged these expectations, and his reputation was naturally to suffer most from their shortfall.

In this situation, with a perilous shortage of supplies aggravated every day now by the Axis failure to take Malta, Rommel had at all costs to try to avoid a reversion to that static warfare, in which, he said, victory 'goes to the side with the most ammunition'. While he was at the end of the 'elastic', that side would clearly not be the Germans. So, in the last days of August, he decided to try one final attack, this time against the new opponents, Alexander and Montgomery. They had virtually accepted the entire defensive plan bequeathed them by Auchinleck, which involved defending the position at El Alamein and round the ridge of Alam El Halfa, fifteen miles to its south. The ensuing battle, which was, strictly speaking, the second, and middle, battle of El Alamein, is called the battle of Alem El Halfa, because the ridge became the key feature in

OPPOSITE An Africa Corps Panzer rolling menacingly towards the east and the enemy, through the narrow street of a Libyan coastal town. A propaganda picture of North Africa as the German popular imagination no doubt conceived it.

Fierce fighting continued by
the lurid light of flares
and explosions.

the British defence. In fact, the Axis attack was to fail, but
when the British showed no inclination to exploit the victory
and pursue Rommel westwards, he also settled down into a
defensive position opposite them – a return to the static warfare he so feared and hated – and both sides then prepared and
waited for the set-piece engagement of late October, when the
third and last battle at El Alamein was joined.

On the morning of 30 August, the day on which the attack
was to start, Rommel is said to have emerged from his sleep-
ing-truck with a very troubled face and confronted his doctor,

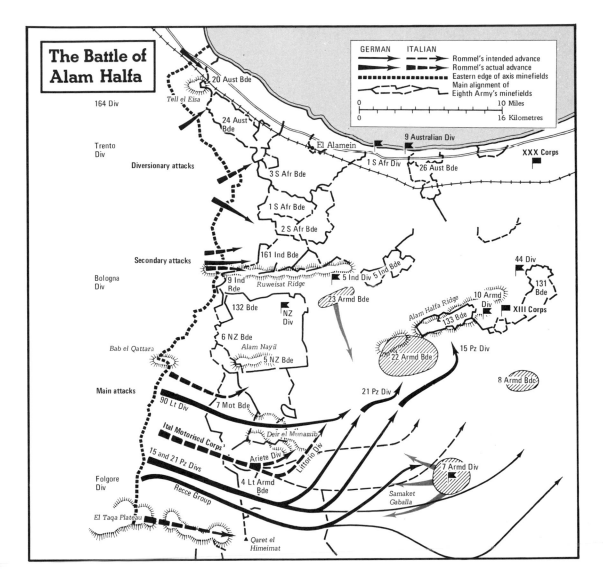

The Battle of Alam Halfa

GERMAN   ITALIAN

⮕ ⇢ Rommel's intended advance
⇢ ⇢ Rommel's actual advance
▪▪▪▪ Eastern edge of axis minefields
〰️ Main alignment of Eighth Army's minefields

0 ——————— 10 Miles
0 ——————— 16 Kilometres

164 Div

20 Aust Bde
Tell el Eisa

24 Aust Bde

Trento Div

Diversionary attacks

El Alamein

9 Australian Div

XXX Corps

3 S Afr Bde

1 S Afr Div

26 Aust Bde

1 S Afr Bde

2 S Afr Bde

161 Ind Bde

44 Div

131 Bde

Secondary attacks

9 Ind Bde

5 Ind Div 5 Ind Bde

Bologna Div

Ruweisat Ridge

23 Armd Bde

10 Armd Div

XIII Corps

132 Bde

NZ Div

Alam Halfa Ridge

133 Bde

6 NZ Bde

Alam Nayil

15 Pz Div

Bab el Qattara

5 NZ Bde

22 Armd Bde

8 Armd Bde

Main attacks

21 Pz Div

90 Lt Div

7 Mot Bde

Ital Motorised Corps

Deir el Munassib

15 and 21 Pz Divs

Ariete Div

Littorio Div

7 Armd Div

Folgore Div

Recce Group

4 Lt Armd Bde

Samaket Gaballa

El Taqa Plateau

▲ Qaret el Himeimat

Professor Horster, with the words, 'the decision to attack today is the hardest I have ever taken. Either the army in Russia succeeds in getting through to Grozny and we in Africa manage to reach the Suez canal, or . . . .' He then made a gesture of defeat. His plan of attack was simple and predictable, since, like so many of the desert battles, there were very few alternative choices to be made. The reason so many of Rommel's attacks were successful is not that they contained any unexpected initial plan of attack, but that, in spite of being predictable, they were executed through the initial and earlier

163

phases with such improbable daring and speed that their subsequent course became unpredictable, and it was then that Rommel's genius for instant improvisation and inventiveness came into its own.

At Alam Halfa, with his much reduced and vastly inferior forces, Rommel had no real alternative but to try to go round behind the left of the British flank, in a thirteen-mile gap left between its southern end and the Qattara depression. Then, as usual, he hoped to sweep his Panzers northwards and engage in a fast-moving, swirling armoured battle with no shape – the kind of battle in which he and his troops were at their best, while the more slowly reacting British troops and commanders were at their worst. While his armour was penetrating in the south, the Italian divisions would be attacking the British defences all the way along the fifteen-mile line northwards to the coast. As usual, Rommel's plan had an almost impossible time-scale, and this was one of the first things to go wrong.

The night advance of his mobile thrust to the south foundered on the fact that, owing to faulty reconnaissance, it took much longer than expected to get through the British minefields which had been laid across the gap between the Qattara depression and the southernmost British position. The result was that the speed and surprise essential to Rommel's plan were lost. Ronald Lewin in his book *Rommel as Military Commander* noted that the battle 'had been lost in the first few hours'. At the height of his powers, Rommel would not only have sensed this, but would have produced a radical innovation either to mitigate the effects or to overturn the circumstances and produce a different verdict. This time, for once, his intuition seemed to have left him. Sickness, exhaustion and perhaps the beginning of a much deeper despair which becomes evident later on, already seemed to have affected his normally over-developed flair for improvisation; Kesselring noticed that the 'iron determination to persevere was lacking' and commented later that, without it, the gamble of the attack should never have been taken on. He decided to seek advice from General Bayerlein, who had then taken over command of the Africa Corps when its own commander had been wounded. They decided to go on – though there was nothing much they could do now that they had lost the freedom of manœuvre.

Whichever way they advanced, the Africa Corps would

A unique documentation of war in the desert: Wilhelm Wessel, commissioned by a British regiment (The 3rd King's Own Hussars) portrays an incident during the siege of Tobruk, 1941. Featured are German Mark IV Panzers opposing Mark VI B Light Tanks of the British regiment.

become exposed on their flanks. If they advanced northwards, they would confront the 10th Armoured Division and the heavily fortified defences on the ridge of Alam Halfa, with the 7th Armoured Division coming in at them from the east; if they advanced east, they would face the 7th Armoured Division. Since, by then, Rommel's divisions were probably weaker than each British brigade – let alone a division – he could hardly afford to assault the Alam Halfa position. Moreover, the Africa Corps' fuel and ammunition was desperately short, too short for any plan which involved a protracted slugging match, or much manœuvring. There was fuel available for only one day's driving – an average of sixty-two miles – while a five-hundred-ton consignment, which had been promised for that day by Kesselring, failed to arrive simply because most of it was consumed by the convoys bringing it on the seven-day round-trip from Benghazi. Moreover, Montgomery, fully conscious of these shortages, ordered his men to concentrate their attacks on Rommel's 'soft-skinned' vehicles – his supply columns.

'Montgomery ordered his men to concentrate their attacks on Rommel's "soft-skinned" vehicles – his supply columns'

Rommel again considered whether or not to break off the battle. His position was deteriorating under the merciless British bombing, which had Rommel himself running for cover six times during the day. For the first time, he was suffering from a clear-cut enemy supremacy in the air, which made a most marked impression on him and was to play a very large part in his attitude to the D-day landings in Normandy two years later. Rommel complained to Kesselring about the bombing. The latter promised to do something about it, but on the night of 2 September, Rommel's forces were once again subjected to a non-stop pounding by British bombers, illuminating their targets with a steady succession of flares and incendiaries.

It was enough. On 3 September, the German withdrawal began. Montgomery had originally ordered preparations for a counter-stroke, but in the event, the Germans were given a whole day to get their withdrawal underway, and by the time the counter-attack came, it was a muddled, inconclusive affair. For the next two days, Rommel was able to pull his men out without hindrance, for Montgomery decided to break off the battle, presumably to conserve his men for a later date at which his superiority in numbers, and preparedness in training, would be so much greater that victory would be indisputable.

A dwindling German fuel
store at El Alamein.

It is arguable that if Montgomery had ordered a counter-
attack and pursuit at that particular moment, he might then
have been able to finish off the Africa Corps for good. Certainly it is a tempting speculation, since it is now known in
what a parlous state Rommel's forces were. Such a course
would have pre-empted the subsequent build-up which was
to occur on both sides during the next six weeks, and might
thus have shortened the war in North Africa. But Montgomery
was not appointed to the command of the 8th Army to take
chances. The whole essence of his strategy was that he would
not move forward until he was absolutely certain of victory.
This made for caution and dullness, to be sure, arousing
the occasional contempt of the more imaginative Rommel.
But, before the end, he had recognised the soundness of

The Retreat of the Afrika Korps

Rommel's decision to get out from El Alamein spelt the end of all he had fought for in Africa. It involved a seemingly unending retreat without any hope of relief. It was that much more painful than any of his previous decisions, which may have carried long-term implications of defeat, but did not involve as immediate disaster as this.

ABOVE British infantry rushing the crew of a knocked-out German tank.

LEFT Australian soldiers helping a wounded German at El Alamein, a scene which might have been especially contrived to contradict the belief, common among the Africa Corps, that Australians gave no quarter in battle.

RIGHT A wrecked Italian fighter is inspected by an Allied soldier. Rommel found the inferiority of Axis air power one of his greatest handicaps.

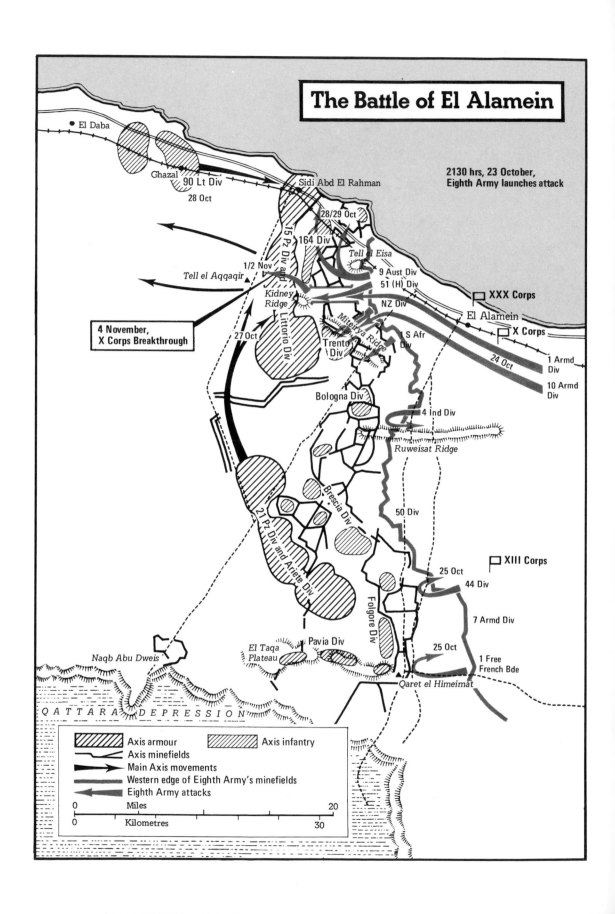

The Battle of El Alamein

2130 hrs, 23 October, Eighth Army launches attack

El Daba

Ghazal

90 Lt Div

28 Oct

Sidi Abd El Rahman

28/29 Oct

15 Pz Div and

164 Div

Tell el Eisa

9 Aust Div

Tell el Aqqaqir

1/2 Nov

51 (H) Div

Kidney Ridge

NZ Div

XXX Corps

El Alamein

X Corps

4 November, X Corps Breakthrough

27 Oct

Littorio Div

Meteirya Ridge

1 S Afr Div

Trento Div

24 Oct

1 Armd Div

10 Armd Div

Bologna Div

4 Ind Div

Ruweisat Ridge

Brescia Div

50 Div

21 Pz Div and Ariete Div

XIII Corps

25 Oct

44 Div

Folgore Div

7 Armd Div

Naqb Abu Dweis

El Taqa Plateau

Pavia Div

25 Oct

1 Free French Bde

Qaret el Himeimat

Q A T T A R A   D E P R E S S I O N

Axis armour		Axis infantry

Axis minefields

Main Axis movements

Western edge of Eighth Army's minefields

Eighth Army attacks

0   Miles   20

0   Kilometres   30

Montgomery's strategy even if he retained a low opinion of him as a tactician.

After the battle of Alam Halfa, both armies settled down to a six-week 'battle of supplies'. Rommel knew that an enormous convoy carrying 100,000 tons of supplies was due to reach the British in September. But, after Alam Halfa, he did not have the strength to do much about it. All he could do was to wrestle unsuccessfully with his own supply difficulties. He complained that it never proved possible to take the Malta fortress, and even disclosed that he offered then to do it himself. Perhaps he had forgotten the very different emphasis that he had been putting on the capture of Malta in the euphoria after Tobruk in June.

In September, he demanded 30,000 tons and another 35,000 tons for October as the minimum supplies needed if his African army was to stand any chance of neutralising the forthcoming British attack. Less than half had arrived when the battle was again joined in late October. His appeals fell on German ears deafened by the mighty battle of Stalingrad which even at that moment hung in the balance. It is quite likely also that – Stalingrad apart – the German High Command were less susceptible to Rommel's appeals than they might have been, because so often in the past he had proved himself capable of military successes which defied all the accepted laws of logistics. Why should he not do it again? According to Ciano in Rome, Mussolini was also angry with him for accusing Italian officers of leaking his plans to the British. 'As always victory finds a hundred fathers, but defeat is an orphan,' he wrote. There were also rumours in Rome that Kesselring had flown to Berlin to complain of Rommel and that it was possible that he would be recalled.

Eventually, later that month, it was not Rommel's reputation which finally forced a recall from Germany, but his health. Before going on sick leave, he asked Hitler to replace him with General Guderian, who had been suspended after a dispute with his superiors in the Russian campaign. Hitler refused; 'No doubt a piece of luck for me', Guderian remarked later. Instead, Rommel's replacement turned out to be General Stumme, the very man whose Panzer division he had taken over in 1940. On 23 September, he left Stumme 'with a heavy heart', assuring him that he would return if the British opened a major offensive. He went first to Rome, where Mussolini found him 'physically and morally shaken' and was convinced that he would not come back. Then he flew to Hitler's eastern headquarters. In both places, he stressed the importance of air power in the desert and claimed that British air supremacy was one of the main causes of his setbacks. He also warned his leaders that, without the supplies he had asked for, the Africa Corps would not be able to keep going.

Although Halder had by then just been dismissed, Rommel found relations no easier with the remaining members of the High Command. Indeed, the atmosphere was extremely – absurdly – optimistic, perhaps for the very fact that Halder *had* gone. Goering in particular seemed to needle him, when Rommel described how the British fighter-bombers were firing American-made armour-piercing cannon shells into his tanks. Goering said: 'That's impossible. The Americans only know how to make razor blades.' 'We could do with some of those razor blades, *Herr Reichsmarschall*', replied Rommel. He was fobbed off by Hitler with promises which he discovered later – much later – had never had any hope of fulfilment. He then went into the mountains near Vienna for a complete rest.

Although Rommel was absent from Africa during the few weeks before the start of the last battle of El Alamein, the defence plan which he left behind was preserved basically unchanged by General Stumme. Rommel had chosen a static defence, consisting of a line of fixed positions fortified by enormous minefields stretching from the coast to the Qattara depression. He was forced to choose this most uncharacteristic plan for three reasons: first, he had lost so many men from his mechanised divisions that, for once, he had to adopt tactics in which the non-motorised divisions played a more prominent – almost predominant – part; second, British air supremacy thoroughly inhibited his use of mobile formations, so that he was better off in static, well dug-in positions; and third, he was so short of petrol that he could not afford the risk of having to break off in the middle of a mobile defence battle because he had run out of fuel.

He placed all his infantry divisions behind a screen of 500,000 mines, and kept his two Panzer divisions to the rear, separated from each other by about twenty-five miles. This separation of his armour was another unusual decision – again forced on him by the exigencies of the fuel situation. It meant that he was able to use much more of his armour for instant counter-attacks against any place at which the British might

'*Mussolini found him physically and morally shaken*'

ABOVE A German landing strip on the Libyan front. The bright red smoke marker provides a wind-direction guide for incoming aircraft.

RIGHT Warfare in the Western Desert was more like war at sea than on land. Rommel realised this more quickly than the Allies, repeatedly stressing that what mattered was not gaining territory, but the relentless destruction of enemy *matériel*.

break through, and it also meant that, wherever the break-through occurred, he would soon have some armour in the vicinity without using too much fuel.

While Rommel's plan remained unaltered, Montgomery was chopping and changing, and was to do so again during the battle. His final intention shortly before the battle was to punch a hole through Rommel's defences quite close to the coast, with troops from the 30th Corps, while the 13th Corps would be sent forward in the south of the line to make a sec-ondary attack and keep the southern part of Rommel's armour preoccupied. Montgomery's decision to fight the battle in that way meant that it would inevitably turn into a battle of attri-tion – a slugging match – in which, in spite of much heavier losses, the British with their vastly superior numbers would eventually prevail, provided their commander had the will to persevere.

At the start of the battle, the 8th Army's fighting strength was 230,000 men, while Rommel had only 80,000 of whom 27,000 were Germans. Liddell Hart, in his *History of the Second World War*, calculates that the British started with a six-to-one majority in tanks and a much greater capacity to make up their losses. British air superiority was about five to one, though the Royal Air Force had already made its most telling contribution to the battle – even before it started – by the destruction and strangulation of the Axis supply routes from Italy. All through the night of 23 October, British infan-try struggled slowly through the minefields after the attack had been heralded by a fifteen-minute bombardment from a thousand guns. Early the next day, General Stumme decided to drive up to the front unescorted, to see for himself. But he lacked the luck of Rommel. He was never again to be seen alive. When his vehicle came under fire, he leaped out, and though he clung to the side he seems to have died there of a heart attack, falling off without the driver noticing.

That same afternoon, in Austria, Rommel received a tele-phone call from Hitler, who asked him whether he was well enough to return to Africa. Rommel said that he was. He took off the following morning. 'I knew there were no laurels to be earned in Africa', he wrote, having already learned that the troops' deliveries of supplies had fallen well short of his mini-mum demands. Rommel reached his headquarters at dusk on 25 October, after the fighting had been going on for nearly forty-eight hours. He found that the British had by then

Trucks carrying Allied infantry edge through a gap in an enemy minefield.

driven a short wedge through the minefield, but that its front was extremely narrow and the British had paid dearly for this modest advance. In the south, the secondary attack by the 13th Corps had been abandoned. On the next day, the British again suffered from an attempt to ram their armour through such a narrow gap cleared in the minefield. A tremendous slugging-match ensued round the area of the breach, with German anti-tank defences taking a heavy toll. However, though the Germans managed to contain the British break-out, they could not afford the losses this involved, whereas the British, even with their greater losses, had many more reinforcements behind.

By the third day, Montgomery realised that he was making insufficient headway and changed his plan. On the night of the 28th, he started a new attack due north from his wedge, in an attempt to reach the coast and encircle those Axis defenders who would then be between him and the minefield. This plan also miscarried. It was clear then to Rommel that he should wait no longer for a decisive breakthrough, which could not be long postponed, but should pull out before it came. But he was induced to stay on a little longer by the realisation that, when he did retreat, he would have to leave his non-motorised units behind him. The shortage of petrol meant that the retreat, when it came, could not be a fighting withdrawal, but would involve total disengagement and a straight leap backwards to

175

The elation of these soldiers of a German rifle regiment, exulting in
their capture of Tobruk, was not to last. In a few short months the trap
of El Alamein would be sprung.

176

a new defensive position. There was no question of mobile defence, still less of taking his non-motorised units with him. They would have to make their way back as best they could. The decision clearly spelled the end of all he had fought for in Africa. Since it involved such a seemingly unending retreat – was there no hope of any relief? – it was that much more painful than any of his previous decisions, which may have carried long-term implications of defeat but did not involve an immediate disaster of this kind.

When Montgomery's coastward thrust failed, he went back to his first plan and attacked once more through the wedge on 2 November. Again his tanks were caught by the Germans, and suffered severely. But however badly the British suffered, the sheer process of attrition was working in their favour. Although they started the battle with a six-to-one majority in tanks, and though in that first week they lost hundreds more than the Germans, by 2 November, their superiority had risen to about twenty to one.

On the night of the 2nd, Rommel decided to withdraw to Fuka. 'The dead are lucky. It's all over for them', he wrote to Lu. He intended to break off and fight as many delaying actions as he could on the long retreat west, until either he had recovered his strength enough to hold the 8th Army in one position, or else had covered the retreat successfully enough to enable German troops to be evacuated entirely from Africa. There was no question in Rommel's mind that the logical outcome of his defeat was the Axis evacuation of Africa. But it was not a certainty which he found that his leaders shared – then, or at any time, until the end.

On 3 November, the day after he had started his withdrawal, he received a cable from Hitler insisting that the position must be held to the last man. 'As to your troops, you can show them no other road but victory or death', the Führer concluded. Rommel was shattered. So was everybody else in the Africa Corps. For the first time in Africa, Rommel confessed that he did not know what to do. He says that a kind of apathy came over his staff. Always a stickler for obedience from his own juniors, Rommel obeyed his Führer with a leaden heart. It so happened that Field Marshal Kesselring arrived at Rommel's headquarters on the 4th, and they discussed Hitler's order. Rommel initially accused Kesselring of being indirectly responsible for it, by allowing the Luftwaffe to send back optimistic reports which formed the basis for Hitler's wild

It is perhaps in his long, wearing retreat that Rommel's mettle shows most clearly. He kept the morale of his troops remarkably high by his own participation in all their trials.

misreading of the situation. Kesselring denied this, but said that he thought that Rommel, as the man on the spot, should do what he thought right – in other words, ignore it. Disobedience on that scale was something quite alien to Rommel – it went against the ingrained habit of a lifetime in uniform – and he clearly felt instinctively reluctant to accept Kesselring's advice. He was to discover only later that in this kind of order – many more were to follow as Germany's fortunes receded – Hitler was considering more the requirements of propaganda than those of military necessity. 'Until this moment we in Africa had always had complete freedom of action', Rommel wrote. 'Now that was over.'

Without Hitler's message, Rommel would have had one more day in which to organise his retreat and perhaps make an effective stand farther west at one of the recognised defensive

178

positions which the two armies had fought over so many times already. His compliance with it, even for only twenty-four hours, meant that his retreat, when it came, was saved from being a rout only by the incredible speed with which he executed it, and the enormous bounds which he made between stands. By 4 November, the British breach was at last so wide that the 7th Armoured Division was able to pass through, and it did not matter what Hitler had said about standing fast. His 'death or glory' order became so much waste paper to be left behind with the rest of the baggage, as the Africa Corps took to its heels. 'So now it had come – our front broken and the fully motorised enemy streaming into our rear. Superior orders could no longer count. We had to save what there was to be saved', wrote Rommel. He issued orders for the retreat to start immediately. Twenty-four hours later, a signal arrived from the Führer, authorising a withdrawal. Rommel later asserts that the twenty-four-hour delay after Hitler's first order came through was his only mistake, and robbed him of the opportunity of saving his non-motorised – largely Italian – infantry in a battle-worthy condition.

'*So now it had come – our front broken and the fully motorised enemy streaming into our rear. . . . We had to save what there was to be saved*'

Once again, after the battle, Rommel's luck held. This time it took the form of exceptional caution on the part of Montgomery, which deprived the British of an opportunity to cut off and destroy the entire Axis army. Each time the British forces wheeled round in a left-hook to cut off the retreating Axis forces, their turning circle was too small and the enemy escaped the trap. It happened at Daba on the 5th, and it happened again at Fuka the next day. Then, towards nightfall, heavy rain started to fall between the escarpment and the coast. Rommel was saved. In fact, for many years afterwards, the rain was claimed to be the main reason for Rommel's escape, but Liddell Hart makes a different judgement: 'In analysis it becomes clear that the best opportunities had already been forfeited before the rain intervened – by too narrow moves, by too much caution, by too little sense of the time-factor, by unwillingness to push on in the dark, and by concentrating too closely on the battle to keep in mind the essential requirements of its decisive exploitation.'

Throughout his long retreat back to Tunisia, Rommel was to exploit these shortcomings in his opponents' tactics so successfully that it is hard to believe how few troops he had fighting against the massive and deliberate advance of the 8th Army. His divisions were often down to fewer than ten tanks

Beaching guns before the Torch expedition. This was the first Allied amphibious landing at Surcouf in Morocco in November 1942. American troops manhandle the guns whilst the British look on.

each, and his total fighting strength was about 7,500 men in all – 5,000 Germans and 2,500 Italians – against at least twenty times that number. Yet, at each stage of the withdrawal, after each leap backwards, he stayed just long enough to force the British to start ponderously limbering up for an assault on his position – before he slipped away once again. On 7 November, he left Mersah Matruh; on the 9th, Sollum and Halfaya, where he had to abandon a forty-mile column of about a thousand vehicles jammed in the narrow passes and suffering terribly from British bombing. The British were ever wary of his potential for savage counter-attacks – though this time they were surely guilty of a gross over-estimate of his strength. Nevertheless, each time he stopped, they too stopped for reinforcements, to make doubly, trebly – almost infinitely – sure of their ability to take him on. And then, he was gone again before they had the chance. On 26 November, Rommel reached Mersa Brega, where he was marginally reinforced by Italian infantry. The British took two weeks to build up their assault, which was planned for 14 December. On the night of the 12th, Rommel slipped away to Buerat, 250 miles to the west. The British lumbered up once again. This time, their preparations for an assault took a month.

Yet there was never any doubt in their minds what the eventual outcome was going to be. On 8 November, Rommel

General von Arnim following his capture, on arrival at an Allied Camp near Algiers in May 1943.

had heard that an Anglo-American landing had been made in north-west Africa. He too had no illusions. 'This spelt the end of the army in Africa', he said. And to Lu he wrote: 'What will become of the war if we lose North Africa? How will it finish? I wish I could get free of these terrible thoughts.' While Rommel continued to retreat into Tripolitania, the British and American forces started to plan their first offensive against Tunisia, which started on 25 November. It stumbled forward, 'violating every recognised principle of war', as its supreme commander, General Eisenhower, wrote at the time. The result of its failures in December meant that the moment would be delayed at which Rommel's army would be trapped between an enemy threat from both east and west. It also meant that Hitler and Mussolini had time to send out reinforcements to Tunisia, in the form of a new Panzer army under General von Arnim; this made Rommel very jealous, but, in fact, its ultimate effect was only to enlarge the prisoner-of-war pens when the Axis forces surrendered the following May.

But the Anglo-American force advancing eastwards was not the only trouble in Rommel's rear. That danger was to come a few weeks later when they threatened to cut off Rommel and prevent him linking up with the German army in northern Tunisia. But, throughout his retreat, Rommel was also at loggerheads with his political masters. Convinced that hostile colleagues were undermining his reputation at headquarters, Rommel flew to the Führer at his base in east Prussia. He found a noticeable chill in the atmosphere there. Undeterred, or perhaps insensitive to the art of dealing with politicians – even those who were most hysterical – he spoke his mind about the shortages in Africa and recommended that, since supplies were obviously not going to be forthcoming, the African theatre should be abandoned as a long-term policy. At this, Hitler flew into a fury. Rommel 'began to realise that he [Hitler] simply did not want to see the situation as it was, and that he reacted emotionally against what his intellect told him was right'. Hitler told him to hang on, and sent him to Rome with Goering, who would see that everything was done to bring him the required supplies. This can have been no joy to Rommel. He hated Goering, his 'bitterest enemy', whom he suspected of trying to get him dismissed in Africa. Rommel proposed to Goering that he should retreat right back to the Gabes line, but Goering would not hear of it. In a conference with Mussolini, Goering accused Rommel of deserting the

181

Italians at El Alamein. To Rommel's surprise and pleasure, Mussolini chipped in to his defence: 'That's news to me,' he said, 'your retreat was a masterpiece, Marshal Rommel.'

However, Mussolini was not always so accommodating. The loss of Italy's African empire was a political disaster for him from which he might never recover. For Rommel, on the other hand, Tripolitania, which was the jewel of that empire, was merely another space to be used or surrendered according to military necessity and logistic possibility. And those necessities were primarily German. Friction was inevitable.

When Rommel reached Buerat, Mussolini appeared to be taking a cue from Hitler and signalled him with an order to resist 'to the utmost' there. This was not what Rommel had planned. For him the next natural and reasonably secure defence line was at Gabes, miles behind him across the Tunisian border. He appealed to Cavallero, Mussolini's Foreign Minister, that Buerat was not a real defensive position, and was eventually allowed to sidle away on the eve of the British assault. He finally brought all his troops into what was known as the Mareth line, east of Gabes, on 22 January. It was from here that Rommel's last six weeks in Africa were to see a final spasm of offensive action, but were to be discoloured by continuous bickering with his colleagues, and two decisive defeats, one each at the hands of the two Allied wings closing in on him.

Rommel was technically removed from his command on 26 January, when he received a signal from the Italian High Command saying that, on account of his bad health, he would be released from his command at a date to be left to his own discretion. His first reaction was to say the sooner the better. He told Lu that it was not for health reasons, but principally for prestige reasons, that he was being removed, though he did also admit to feeling unwell, suffering from headaches, overstrain, circulation troubles and insomnia. His successor designate, the Italian General Messe, arrived at the beginning of February.

After this spontaneous but rather petulant reaction, however, Rommel soon developed a reluctance to take his dismissal lying down. Contrary to the advice of his doctor, he decided to stay where he was until he was ordered to go. Not only did he not feel able to tear himself away from 'his Africans', he also saw an opportunity for a final attempt to seize back the initiative before the two wings of the Allied forces closed in on him and on von Arnim's army in the north. Unfortunately, the plan which Rommel devised to restore the Axis fortunes relied for its success on the fusion of effort between his army group and von Arnim's army; but, owing to the clash of personalities involved, this was impossible to achieve. Kesselring, between and above the two feuding army commanders, tried his best to achieve some co-ordination, but the eventual result was that they operated with only the minimum of co-operation. Misunderstandings arose – 'pigheadedness' by both of them according to Kesselring – and whereas Rommel on his own, with complete authority and complete freedom of action, might have pulled off a spectacular *coup* in the two battles of Kasserine and Medenine, the effect of his bad health, the long dispiriting retreat and the mutual antipathy between him and von Arnim all conspired to send him out of Africa with two distinctive defeats immediately behind him.

Rommel's plan was to take advantage of Montgomery's laborious preparations at the Mareth line to turn on the Allies advancing eastward into Tunisia from Algeria, savage them in the mountains on the frontier and then return to the coastal plain to deal with Montgomery. The Anglo-American force was already threatening to come down through the mountain

Mobility was the key to survival in Rommel's gruelling retreat. But at Kasserine Rommel halted to make a counter-thrust at his pursuers.

passes and endanger Rommel's right flank if he continued his retreat round the coast to Tunis. Rommel intended to penetrate those passes and drive up in a north-westerly direction to a depth which would totally disrupt the enemy's rear. The logic of his plan relied on the closest co-ordination between his forces attacking through the passes from the south, and von Arnim's coming in from the north. However, von Arnim demurred, and eventually Kesselring had to work out a compromise which, in effect, meant two different operations with a much less ambitious plan.

The battle of Kasserine started on 14 February with Axis thrusts into Allied forward positions which were immediately successful, unbalancing the inexperienced American units and causing heavy losses. Rommel soon wanted to exploit this victory as best he could, and press on to capture Tebessa, which would have caused the Allies to think seriously of withdrawing back into Algeria. He said later that, though never before had he gambled with his troops – a highly questionable statement from a man who had fought consistently against vastly superior opponents with the minimum of support – he now decided that he must push on hard, at the risk of losing everything.

For a brief moment, the adrenalin of a mobile and offensive battle started to work its old magic on Rommel's imagination. The deep, almost impregnable pessimism of the last few months momentarily evaporated. His narrative bristles once again with the old self-confidence. Rommel lay with his troops in the fighting line. He appeared in the battle area to cheer on a new division in the course of their attack, and to be cheered back by the admiring soldiers. His ADC later reported to Lu that, on the first evening of the battle, he ordered a bottle of champagne and said that he felt like an old warhorse that had heard music again. Under the tonic influence of the battle, even his doctor agreed that there was no harm now in a postponement of the necessary treatment.

But alas, the moment was short-lived. Still von Arnim held back. Rommel therefore appealed to Rome for his more ambitious plan. He was given a rather loose overall command, but only for an operation which again fell short of his original intention to make a decisive thrust into the Allied rear areas. He pressed forward once again on 19 February, but continued to suffer from either misunderstanding or downright dilatoriness on von Arnim's part. Although he captured the Kasserine

ABOVE Rommel's initial
minor gains at the
Kasserine Pass gave him a
new attacking spirit.

RIGHT Despite Rommel's
hopes, von Arnim and his
Panzer reinforcements never
reached the Kasserine front.
The Germans were dis-
astrously outnumbered, and
Rommel broke off the battle.

pass on the 20th, the attack petered out and by the 22nd, he and Kesselring had agreed that the weight of Allied reinforcements inhibited much further exploration through to Thala, which had been Rommel's real objective. It was a resigned but dispirited Rommel who ordered his troops to break off the attack and return first to Gafsa and then to face the 8th Army again in the Mareth line.

The early stages of the battle had produced all the electrifying features of the old Rommel, the fighting animal. Had he been able to persevere with his attack, he might have achieved his strategic objective of forcing the Anglo-American forces out of Tunisia. He came close to it; but as with so many of Rommel's African operations, the very closeness to strategic victory which his early tactical successes brought him – before failing to achieve it – magnified the extent of the tactical defeat which followed. So it was at Kasserine. Ironically, the day after his withdrawal, he was appointed Supreme Commander over a new formation called Army Group Africa which was to contain all the Axis troops there, both his and von Arnim's. In his now renewed depression, he refused the job. He had had enough. But, the next day, the appointment came through regardless, and Rommel was forced to accept.

If the group had been formed earlier, Rommel would have been able to integrate von Arnim's forces fully into his planning for the battle of Kasserine. Possibly he could then have achieved the decisive result which was bound to elude the two wings of the German forces operating at one remove from each other. The second leg of his double attack was against Montgomery in the Mareth line at Medenine. It was already too late. If it had been mounted one week earlier, even with his much depleted forces, he would have found Montgomery in a surprisingly weak position with little more than one division in the line. But by the time Rommel did attack, on 6 March, the British had increased their forces to four times that number, in a strongly defended position. Rommel was immediately outgunned, and was forced to call off the attack on the first evening.

He was a sick man, and a defeated Field Marshal. He complained to Lu that he thought that his nerves would snap. There was nothing left for him here. Three days after Medenine, he handed over his command to General von Arnim, and flew to Hitler to try to persuade the Führer of the hopelessness of the Axis position in Africa. He never returned.

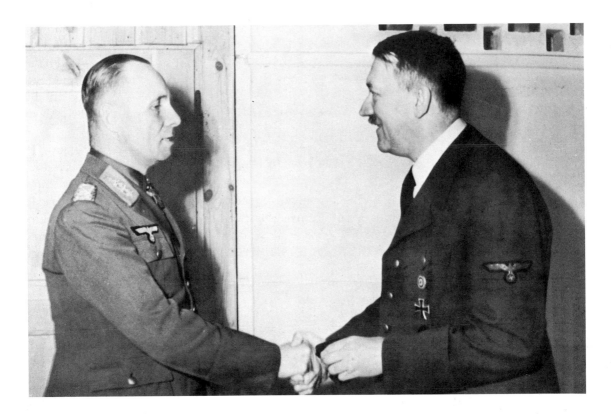

Hitler adds the highest decoration, Oak Leaves with Swords and Diamonds, to Rommel's Knight's Cross of the Iron Cross. Ironically, this recognition of his services in Africa came at a time when he was a sick and defeated man with little faith left in his *Führer*.

Rommel by then was recommending a complete withdrawal from Africa while there was still time, or, failing that, a shorter line of defence round the northern end of Tunisia. Perhaps his reputation for pessimism invalidated such arguments from him even before they were put. Anyway, Hitler was unrelenting. Africa was to be held. He ordered Rommel on sick leave, turning down his entreaties to be allowed back (did Rommel really want to go back by then?) with the sweetener – absurd by then to anyone, but most absurd of all to Rommel – that he would be allowed back for the operations against Casablanca! He decorated Rommel with the highest order of the Iron Cross – oakleaves with swords and diamonds – and insisted on the utmost secrecy being preserved about Rommel's recall from Africa. With or without him, however, the end for his troops in Africa was to be the same. Inexorably, the Allied forces closed in on them until by 13 May, virtually the whole Axis force – nearly 200,000 men – had surrendered. Three days before this final disaster, Hitler summoned Rommel to Berlin and confessed: 'I should have listened to you before. But I suppose it's too late now.' It was indeed.

187

8
Invasion
and End

ROMMEL'S DEPARTURE FROM AFRICA was not the prelude to a long period of disgrace. His relations with both the dictators – Hitler and Mussolini – were subject to violent and frequent oscillations, but the fact that Rommel was never for long in disfavour with his masters was not attributable solely to his capacity to win back their support with a quick success on the battlefield, nor to their mercurial temperaments. The other factor was that there was never any question of Rommel being anything other than a plain soldier – a dogmatic, difficult soldier certainly, and one who seemed to find it increasingly hard to work with any of his equals or superiors who disagreed with him – but a soldier, none the less, without any politics in him. It made him at times unwelcome to his masters, but not unpopular in the sense in which his prickly and exaggerated military egocentrism made him unpopular with his fellow marshals.

But one thing which the dictators seemed to feel they could rely on was that Rommel would be predictable and loyal, however difficult for him that loyalty might prove to be. In this they were very nearly right, for Rommel *was* predictable, and even when, in 1944, he became peripherally connected with some of the plotting to eliminate Hitler, his motive then – which never moved him to take positive action himself, but only to condone tacitly what others were doing and saying – was that the war was being lost. After the six years of close and stormy relations with Hitler, he came to object to him because he was losing the war and was mad and bad enough not to care, not because he was just generally mad and bad. If Hitler had not then been losing the war by his decisions, it might have been a different story.

Hitler's feelings towards Rommel were also generally benign until the final suspicions overwhelmed him in the hysteria which followed the unsuccessful attempt on his life in July 1944. Rommel had clearly appealed to the Führer ever since they first met. Rommel's plain ways probably comforted Hitler, whose paranoia so often persuaded him that he was surrounded by plotters – as indeed he frequently was. Even after the storms and disagreements over Africa, when Rommel returned to Europe and was subsequently given a command in the Italian theatre, Kesselring complained of Hitler's fascination for Rommel, that he was 'hypnotised' by Rommel's ideas and showed an almost 'obsequious submissiveness' to him, much to Kesselring's disgust.

PREVIOUS PAGES Rommel's coffin is carried with all due State ceremony through the town of Ulm, near his home.

Back in Germany, away from his troops, Rommel was a misfit, although his influence with Hitler was still considerable. This informal picture shows him with Propaganda Minister Goebbels's four daughters, later to be poisoned by their parents in the Führer's bunker in Berlin during the last days of the Reich.

It is not surprising therefore that soon after the African débâcle, Hitler attached Rommel to his own staff, thus relieving him of the 'unbearable loneliness' which he had felt after leaving Africa. While he was on Hitler's staff he obviously came to know the Führer better than ever before and had several long talks with him. In these, Rommel appeared to have broached what most of Hitler's generals would surely have regarded as the great unmentionable – the possibility of German defeat. In spite of the enormous mobilisation of German resources which really only started to get underway in 1943, Germany could not eventually 'keep pace with the whole world', he told the Führer. Hitler appeared, this time at least, to take what he said in an almost philosophical mood, agreeing with the premise but concluding that the West would never agree to peace with him. On another occasion, a very different Hitler blurted out angrily to him 'If the German people are incapable of winning the war, they can rot.' The best were already dead, he said; a great people must die heroically – it was a historic necessity. Rommel later told his son, 'Sometimes you feel that he's no longer quite normal.'

191

On 10 July, Rommel's fairly dull summer was broken by the Allied landings in Sicily, and in early September they went on to land in southern Italy. Hitler had clearly toyed with the idea of putting Rommel in command of all Axis forces in Italy, and was to flirt with this thought again, but for the moment it did not materialise. In July, he was sent instead to Greece in preparation for an appointment there as Commander-in-Chief of all forces in the area. He was recalled as rapidly as he had been despatched, by news from Italy which came as a totally unexpected blow to Hitler's plans.

Mussolini had been deposed. The Italian situation, both internal and with regard to the Axis alliance, was confused and uncertain. Rommel was to take command of an army group in the Alps and prepare for a possible entry into Italy, either to occupy the country or to stiffen its backbone against possible desertion from the Axis. He was personally ordered not to set foot in Italy, as his presence there might have proved provocative. So he fretted on the frontier while Hitler and the Allies competed for Italy's soul. Mussolini was not likely to come back, he told Lu, but this was not necessarily a disadvantage: 'It suits us in some ways, of course, to have only one big man running things in Europe.' His own 'big man', however, continued to forbid him to enter Italy.

The Allies landed in Italy on 4 September, and the Italians signed an armistice on the 8th. Rommel, speaking bitterly of their treachery, was taken off for an appendix operation. When he recovered in October, he returned, still hoping to get the supreme command in the south. There is every sign that Hitler did indeed intend to appoint him to supreme command of the Italian theatre with charge of both his own forces and those of Kesselring. But while the order confirming this appointment was being transmitted, Hitler changed his mind and appointed Kesselring. Rommel was given a totally new task as Inspector General of the Atlantic wall defences against an Allied invasion across the Channel, which by then everyone realised was bound to come.

From November 1943 until July 1944, Rommel was to be totally preoccupied first with the defensive preparations for and then with the battle against the Allied invasion of Normandy, which took place on 6 June 1944. For the first two months as Inspector General, he was in the uneasy position of having responsibility without power. He had been deputed to inspect the state of the coastal defences, but possessed neither

Disappointed in his hopes of the Italian command, Rommel none the less threw himself vigorously into the bleak task of strengthening the defences on the Atlantic Wall.

193

Rommel's research into coastal defence preparations led to some rather disquieting findings, and he energetically set about organising improvements like the concrete fort behind him in this picture.

the staff nor the established authority to do much about it, since the area came under the command of Field Marshal von Runstedt, the Commander-in-Chief West. In spite of these difficulties, Rommel was to achieve enormous improvements in the defences, though even then he was able only to bring them from useless to inadequate. If he had only been able to spend another year on them, the Allies might have found themselves facing a more formidable opposition.

Rommel's position was slightly improved, however, on 31 December 1943, when he was given an army group under von Runstedt, with responsibility for an area stretching from Holland to Bordeaux. This was not fully satisfactory either,

but the two Field Marshals were able to develop quite an adequate working relationship – in spite of, or maybe because of, their great differences in age, personality and background.

Rommel's first analysis of the situation was that the Allies would invade across the Channel in the Pas de Calais, largely because this was the area from which the V-I rockets would be launched against England. He concluded that the only way in which his generally inferior forces could defeat the invasion was by preventing the enemy from developing a major bridge-head from which it could exploit its own superiority. Every effort must therefore be made not to lie back waiting to launch a major counter-attack when the Allies' bridgehead

Builder of the Atlantic Wall

Rommel believed that the Allies would invade across the Channel in the Pas de Calais, mainly because this was the area from which the V-I rockets would be launched against England. He concluded that the only way in which his generally inferior forces could defeat the invasion was to exploit its own superiority.

Every effort was made therefore not to lie back waiting to launch a major counter-attack when the Allies' bridgehead was established, but to contain them as near to the coast as possible. He ordered a swathe of fortifications to be built along the entire coast – shore batteries, minefields and foreshore obstacles on the beaches. By May 1945, he had organised the construction of 517,000 obstacles, such as the iron stakes which impeded landings on the most probable beaches, and over four million mines – not nearly enough, but nearly four times as many as were in place when Rommel started his work.

RIGHT Rommel examining
anti-tank barriers newly set
up under his command.

LEFT *Batterie Todt :* one of
the many concrete block-
houses that Rommel built
along the coast.

BELOW A drawing by
Rommel of the proposed
paratroop and aircraft
landing barriers which he
designed; they were called
'Rommel Asparagus'.

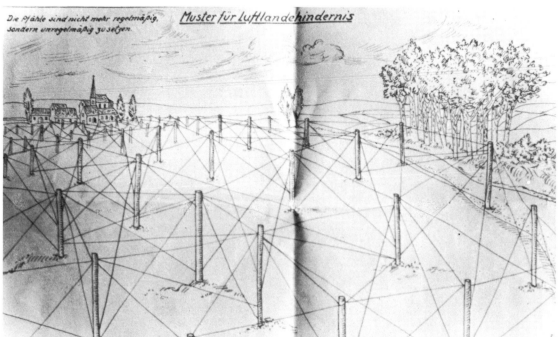

Die Pfähle sind nicht mehr regelmäßig,
sondern unregelmäßig zu setzen.

Muster für Luftlandehindernis

was established, but to contain them as near to the coast as possible. To this end, he ordered a swathe of fortifications to be built along the entire coast – shore batteries, minefields and foreshore obstacles on the beaches. By May 1945, he had organised the construction of 517,000 obstacles, such as the iron stakes which impeded landings on the most probable beaches, and over four million mines – not nearly enough, but nearly four times as many as were in place when Rommel started his work.

Rommel then turned his attention to the kind of tactics which would be required for the land battle after the invasion. He immediately became involved in a typically acrimonious dispute with his fellow commanders. Of all the German commanders at the time, none had suffered so much as Rommel at the hands of enemy airforces. He believed that his colleagues, particularly those with experience of the Russian front, had no conception of the difficulties of having to fight a battle when the enemy had nearly total air supremacy. This dominated his thinking at the time – with a great deal of justification, as events were to show. But at the time it is possible that his colleagues felt that he was exaggerating the effect as a subconscious palliative for his Africa defeat. Indeed, this probably was to some extent true, since the effect of air inferiority in Europe would not be nearly as disastrous, even in a mobile battle, as it obviously was in the pitless open stretches of the desert. Rommel assumed that the Allies' air supremacy would make itself felt on D-Day, and therefore that the policy of holding the Panzer divisions in reserve for a major counter-attack was invalid, because the Allied air attacks would interdict their ability to move forward. The only hope was to keep the armour as close as possible to the likely invasion points, ready for immediate counter-attacks, on the same principles which he had with great effect applied to his armour at El Alamein.

Field Marshal von Runstedt and one of the senior Panzer officers in France, General Geyr von Schweppenburg, held a different view. They wanted to adhere to the more classical doctrine of holding their armour altogether in reserve until it was clear where the main enemy bridgehead was being established, and then concentrate all their reserve in a massive counter-attack. Unfortunately, Rommel's arguments with his colleagues slipped into the familiar pattern of uncompromising disagreement. Even the rehabilitated General Guderian –

German armoured vehicles in a Normandy town smashed by Allied bombing.

doyen of Panzer warfare – with whom Rommel had so much in common, confessed himself unable to make any impression on Rommel's convictions. They met in April 1944, when Guderian and Geyr went to reason with Rommel about his proposed deployment of the armour in small packets close to the coastline. Guderian came away from the encounter saying that Rommel's attitude made argument 'fruitless'. The Field Marshal believed that large land operations were impossible. 'He therefore neither wanted nor tried to organise one', said Guderian. He also found Rommel at the time convinced – and impervious to other arguments – that the Allies would land somewhere near the mouth of the Somme. So Guderian returned to Germany empty handed. Rommel, meanwhile, reported to Lu that he had had to be 'very rough' with General Geyr 'because he would not give way to my plans'. However, orders from above had decided the issue in his favour. The orders came from Hitler, who told the other officers that Rommel had more recent experience than they had.

As usual in his arguments, Rommel tended to get so carried

199

away by the force of his own views that they almost had to become self-fulfilling. Liddell Hart described Rommel's particular brilliance in the fact that, unlike so many soldiers, he combined both forms of military genius, the conceptive and executive. There was a drawback to this too, however. While Rommel held the initiative, his ability to translate his own conceptions into concrete action was invaluable, and at the same time so often ensured his dominance in battle. But when the initiative lay with his opponents, Rommel's conceptive power seemed often to be too dominant, forcing him, as a result of the clarity of his analysis, to accept a much starker situation on the ground than necessarily obtained. In this argument over the Normandy tactics, for instance, his obsession with the great technical resources which America was bringing into the battle seemed to blind him to the essential unpredictability of all war, and certainly to downgrade that very human factor which his own personality had shown was such an essential ingredient in any battle.

On 3 June – three days before the invasion occurred – Rommel had a meeting with von Runstedt and decided, with the latter's permission, to go to Hitler to overcome some of these difficulties. '5th-8th June,' his diary recorded, 'fears of an invasion during this period were rendered all the less by the fact that no amount of air reconnaissance had given the slightest indication that a landing was imminent.' The most urgent need was to get two more Panzer divisions from the Führer. So Rommel, for the third time in his career, was away from his command when the enemy hammer fell upon it. Shortly after midnight on 5 June, Allied paratroops started to land in Normandy, and were followed the next morning by the armada disgorging thousands more men and weapons onto the contested beaches. Rommel was immediately called to the front by his Chief-of-Staff, General Speidel.

The Normandy campaign lasted only five weeks for Rommel. It was his last campaign, and the least satisfactory, for him as much as for historians. He is a long way from the battle-front in his army group. One gets the impression that much more of his energy is directed to fighting high-level battles within the German hierarchy than to the struggle taking place in Normandy. His command is somehow too remote from the actual fighting. There is too little independence – indeed, virtually none. There are too few opportunities of savouring the frenzy of the front line which so obviously

'The Normandy campaign . . . was his last and least satisfactory'

200

inspired Rommel and clearly enhanced his earlier campaigns.

By 10 June, he was telling Lu that there was 'no answer to enemy air superiority'. Three days later he wrote, 'It's time for politics to come into play', presumably meaning peace moves. By then, von Runstedt had come to share his views. Indeed, only about two weeks later, von Runstedt apparently received a telephone call from Field Marshal Keitel, the joint Chief-of-Staff, who asked: 'What shall we do?' 'Do?' replied von Runstedt. 'Make peace, you idiots, what else can you do?' and then hung up. Rommel and von Runstedt tried to bring home the situation to Hitler himself in two meetings, on 17 and 29 June. For the first meeting, Hitler came to Soissons – his last visit to France. Rommel complained of the impossible fighting conditions, and then proposed one final attempt to draw the Allied forces farther south into France before counter-attacking their flanks out of range of support from their naval artillery. Rommel told Lu that Hitler was 'very cordial and in a good humour'. But he was unimpressed with the arguments and left hurriedly the next day with the injunction that victory was to be gained by holding fast to 'every yard of soil'.

The Field Marshals tried again on the 29th, in Germany. The arguments became heated but not explosive. Both soldiers spoke their minds to Hitler, a situation more familiar to Rommel than it was perhaps to von Runstedt. They both expected to be dismissed for it, and von Runstedt was. Perhaps Hitler had so come to expect this from Rommel that he took it from him but not, as something new, from von Runstedt. Perhaps his old faith in Rommel was still working. That kind of talk would, anyway, have made Hitler feel more uncomfortable coming from someone of von Runstedt's age, seniority and patrician background. Perhaps he had heard of the conversation with Keitel.

Field Marshal von Kluge was sent forward to succeed von Runstedt as the Commander-in-Chief West. He arrived at Rommel's headquarters with clearly preconceived views about Rommel's pessimism and insubordination, planted, no doubt, by the mandarins of the general staff. In front of Rommel's own staff, he told him that he would 'now have to get accustomed to carrying out orders' – a strange public conversation to take place between Field Marshals. Rommel was not prepared to put up with this and demanded a written explanation. It was not long – a matter of days – before von

A conference in Paris shortly before the Allied invasion of Normandy. Rommel rarely found himself in agreement with his colleagues: (left to right) von Schweppenburg, Blaskowitz, Sperrle, von Rundstedt, and Krauke.

Kluge had inspected the front and totally accepted the validity of Rommel's analysis of the situation. On 15 July, Rommel sent von Kluge a report which he asked to be forwarded personally to Hitler. It forecast that, owing to the widespread weakness of the German position, they must expect an imminent Allied breakthrough in Normandy. 'The troops are everywhere fighting heroically, but the unequal struggle is nearing its end. It is urgently necessary for the proper conclusion to be drawn from this situation', were the words which he used to end this, his last operational memorandum. Von

Kluge forwarded it to Hitler on 21 July, with a covering note in which he concluded that Rommel's analysis was correct. But, by then, Rommel was not in a position to appreciate the support he had received.

On 17 July, his long run of personal invulnerability was broken. His staff car was attacked by one of those British aircraft whose very freedom to roam the skies over the German lines had caused Rommel such concern. He survived the crash that followed, but only just. His skull was fractured in three places, his cheek-bone destroyed and there were numerous minor wounds, as well as one more serious, in the left eye. While von Kluge was endorsing Rommel's message in effect saying that Germany was defeated, Rommel was fighting, and in the end winning, a much more desperate struggle for his life. But to what end, for both of them? The two Field Marshals were soon to die, von Kluge in five weeks, Rommel in twelve: both by their own hands. But the hand that proffered the poison was the hand of Hitler, remorselessly avenging the attack made on his life on 20 July 1944.

Internal resistance to Hitler had existed in many quarters of Germany throughout most of the time in which he was in power. Even before the war, some of the senior members of the general staff had been plotting to remove Hitler, to prevent him from committing Germany to what they thought would be an ill-advised war. As the blight of the regime spread its poison ever deeper into German society, so resistance was provoked among a variety of groups of people of every political persuasion, and every religion. It was neither a cohesive resistance, nor in the practical – as opposed to the historical – sense was it effective. The most dramatic of these rarely-visible expressions of opposition was the unsuccessful plot to blow Hitler up at his headquarters on 20 July 1944, organised by a wide circle of army officers led by Klaus von Stauffenberg. In the bloody frenzy of its aftermath, Hitler had at least seven thousand suspects arrested, and liquidated about five thousand of them, many of whom had nothing to do with the plot and would have disapproved had they known of it, on the grounds that Hitler's assassination in itself was not going to cure the sickness in German society.

Rommel was a victim of this revenge, as was von Kluge. This did not mean that Rommel was personally active in the mainstream of resistance to Hitler, for he was not. But he *was* connected with it, though in a much more passive way than

203

one would have expected from the severity – and finality – of his punishment. Unfortunately for Rommel, his role was not seen as particularly passive by the plotters – who had a much more ambitious part for him to play in their scheme than he would have dreamed of himself.

Rommel did not come into the conspiracy until very late. It has to be emphasised that, unlike so many others, he was not a plotter in either the moral or political sense of the word. Nor, until very late, was he a plotter even in the patriotic sense, though when he eventually lent himself to the movement and to the idea of deposing Hitler, it was as a patriot and not as a committed anti-Nazi. Of course, he was always unsympathetic to the Nazi machine, from those very early brushes with the party when it impinged on his military perspectives. His natural aversion to politics, and his instinctive fairness and honesty saw to that. But, beyond that, he probably thought about it very little until 1943, when his return to Germany brought him into contact with many fellow officers who were able to tell him of the atrocities committed by the Nazis during the Russian campaign. Probably for the first time, this opened his eyes to the criminal side of Hitler's regime. He was clearly horrified in December 1943 when his son Manfred told him that he wanted to join one of Himmler's SS divisions. 'That's out of the question', he said. When Manfred persisted, Rommel said that he did not want his son to be under the command of a man who was carrying out mass killings. He told Manfred that he had heard that, now the war was not going well, people like Himmler were trying 'by actions of this kind to burn the bridges of the German people behind them'.

At that stage, Rommel probably did not associate Hitler with his suspicions; but, as the evidence mounted in the coming months, he found this exclusion more and more difficult to sustain, until he reached the point at which he implied that he was now ready to associate himself with the plotters, in a modest role, either assisting in the arrest of Hitler, or else consenting to 'play his part' in whatever happened after that. As Terence Prittie says, in *Germans Against Hitler*,

> Rommel was not a true opponent of Nazism, in that he was ready to act only when he judged that Germany's military position was hopeless. But neither was he – as he has often been depicted – a Nazi General and a devoted follower of Hitler's. Although he wanted nothing to do with assassination, he was all in favour of the overthrow of the Nazi regime. He was essentially a patriot, whose

'He was horrified when Manfred told him that he wanted to join one of Himmler's SS divisions'

intellectual capacity was circumscribed and whose understanding of his country's political problems was in no way matched by his military genius. His value to Hitler's opponents would have been very great on July 20.

Rommel's value lay – paradoxically – in the fact that Goebbels' propaganda had built him up into the most popular and widely-known of Hitler's senior generals. His reputation was more or less untarnished as far as the Nazis were concerned, certainly not by the series of dreadful defeats in Russia, nor even by his own African débâcle, which, compared with that in Russia, had not involved many troops; which he had left before the end; and where, for domestic Germany, memories of his more spectacular exploits probably outlasted the agony of his long retreat. Ironically, Rommel's popular reputation with the Nazis probably caused him more damage among many of the plotters. But, owing to the cellular nature of their operations, few of the central figures in the 20 July bomb plot can have known for certain what ambitious plans had been arranged for Rommel – as a full successor to Hitler – by that small group of conspirators who made contact with him early in 1944.

Rommel was first brought into the plotters' world obliquely, by Dr Karl Strolin, a mayor of Stuttgart, who had served with Rommel against the Italians in 1918 and had maintained a close friendship ever since. Strolin had held conversations with Rommel the previous autumn, but it was not until February 1944, in Rommel's own house in Herrlingen, that – during a conversation about the resistance – he cast a real fly on the water and saw Rommel rise to it, not totally, but in a positive rather than a negative manner. He reported back to his main accomplices, General Beck and Carl Goerdeler, mayor of Leipzig, who were altogether more deeply involved in a conspiracy whose tentacles by then stretched right through the German army. This conspiracy had already formulated six plans to assassinate Hitler, but had never managed to bring any of them off. In April 1944, this group of plotters gained an added advantage in that one of their number, General Hans Speidel, was appointed to Rommel's army group as Chief-of-Staff. Without Rommel being fully aware of it, they gradually wove round him a web of expectation and presumption which eventually sent him to his death.

Rommel's despair with Hitler was by then not in doubt, nor was his readiness to accept that it was his duty 'to come to the rescue of Germany'. But, at the time, he was probably not aware that, as far as Goerdeler, Beck and the military governor of Paris, General Stülpnagel, were concerned, his duty would lie in his being installed as temporary president of Germany after Hitler's overthrow, either to conclude some peace with the Anglo-Americans or else, failing that, to use his military prestige to persuade the army in the west virtually to stand aside and let the Allies through, holding the Russian line meanwhile in the east. Indeed, there is some evidence to suggest that Rommel may have been conniving at this or another similar idea in the arrangements which he made for the deployment of his armour after the invasion in Normandy. Guderian complains that, two weeks after the invasion, there were still some Panzer divisions inexplicably stationed round the coast, wasting their strength in battles with Allied warships instead of being moved to confront the invading land forces. Other writers – Generals Speidel and Geyr – suggest that Rommel held back his armour for political reasons, in order to have reliable divisions at hand in preparation for the overthrow of Hitler. It is a fascinating, but alas fruitless, speculation to wonder whether these facts suggest any deeper motives in Rommel's military command at the time. Can the fierce convictions which he was putting so directly on paper in his memoranda to Hitler have been written by a man who at the same time was holding back his strength for these purposes?

There is some additional evidence of an even more intriguing kind from the British side. Rommel, at the time, was being kept under surveillance in his French headquarters not so much by the Gestapo (though he may have been watched by them too) as by a small group of British soldiers from the Special Air Service. They had been parachuted into enemy-held territory to provide long-range intelligence for the Allies. The regularity of Rommel's routine at his headquarters soon made it possible for them to gather all the necessary knowledge about his movements, so that an assassination would have presented no difficulties. The group's leader radioed these facts back to London and asked for permission to finish off the famous Field Marshal. London refused, apparently on two grounds. The first was that British Intelligence already had enough knowledge about the resistance movement to know that Rommel might emerge as a key figure in the event of Hitler's being deposed. The second – allegedly – was that the British by then had made such a close study of Rommel's techniques of command that they felt that they could predict his likely reactions to most tactical situations. In view of this, they were reluctant, by having him killed off, to exchange him for some new and much less predictable commander. If that is a real explanation, it shows that the British had come a long way in their attitudes to Rommel, and in their general confidence when fighting against him, from those dark days in Africa two years before. Perhaps it is a more plausible explanation for the Rommel of 1944 than it would have been for the fighting animal of 1942. By 1944 his keen tactical cutting-edge does seem to have been blunted by events, or perhaps by illness, and certainly by depression. But in the light of what was subsequently known about the resistance movement, it seems that the first explanation for London's sudden concern for Rommel's safety was the more plausible of the two. All these factors reinforce the suspicion that Rommel's final message to Hitler, which von Kluge endorsed, was devised by them as an ultimatum to the Führer to sue for peace, failing which they would feel that their consciences were clear to act.

Rommel does not appear to have had any specific foreknowledge of the 20 July bomb plot, but his accident on 17 July meant that it would not anyway have made much difference to him if he had. When von Stauffenberg failed to blow Hitler up on 20 July, Rommel was lying close to death in a French hospital. On 8 August, he had recovered enough to be removed to his house at Herrlingen, though still a very sick man. In spite of his severe injuries, his physical condition improved rapidly – not so his political condition. On the evening of 20 July, von Stülpnagel, not waiting to hear whether or not the bomb plot had succeeded, rashly went through with his own part and issued orders for the arrest of the Gestapo and ss security police in Paris. It was a hideous mistake, but he realised it too late. The next day, he was summoned to Berlin. On the way, he tried to shoot himself, but succeeded only in destroying his sight. He was rushed to hospital for an emergency operation. When he came round, the first word he uttered was 'Rommel'. It was as good as a death sentence, yet nothing happened immediately. Rommel's convalescence merely continued, if only to make him a fitter man to die.

At Herrlingen, there was an ominous quiet, as all over Germany the plotters one after another were rounded up or disappeared. Rommel was still technically in command of his army group, but no one came to visit him; no one telephoned

'The British were reluctant to have him killed off, to exchange him for some new and much less predictable commander'

Rommel's wife, and behind her, his son Manfred, at the State funeral.

to him; no mention was made of him in the Press. On 6 September, the Rommel family realised that the house was being watched. Rommel told Manfred that they would have to carry pistols with them whenever they went for walks. On 7 October, a few days before Rommel was due to go by car to Tübingen for treatment, he had a message from Keitel summoning him to Berlin for an important interview on the 10th. A special train would be sent for him. Rommel declined to go, on doctor's orders. Five days then went by without a word, while Rommel told one of his closest associates, Admiral Ruge, that he would never go to Berlin. 'I would never get there alive', he said. 'I know they would kill me on the way and stage an accident.'

On 13 October, a telephone call announced that two generals from the personnel division – Burgdorf and Maisel – would call on Rommel at noon the next day. Rommel's reaction to this message was unusually quiet, but if he had fears, he transmitted them to no one. The next day started early. Manfred arrived home on leave at 7 am, and found his father already up. They breakfasted together and went for a long walk. The generals arrived punctually at noon, and were greeted by the whole family, including Rommel's long-standing ADC, Captain Aldinger. The generals went off with Rommel into a downstairs room, while the others went upstairs. In a few moments, Rommel came out and went straight up to see his wife. 'I have come to say goodbye. In a quarter of an hour I shall be dead', he said as he walked into the room. The generals had told him that he was suspected of having taken part in the plot to kill Hitler, and that he was on Goerdeler's government list to succeed Hitler as president of the Reich. Rommel had denied this, but to no avail. Hitler had given him the choice of taking poison and having a state funeral, or going before the People's Court like many of the other accused. There was the added rider that Rommel's family would receive good treatment if he chose the poison, and bad treatment – no pension, and perhaps worse – if he went before the court. Rommel had chosen the poison.

Rommel then told his son and Aldinger. The latter protested that they should at least try to escape, or shoot the two generals. Rommel replied that it was no use. The house was surrounded, and such behaviour would jeopardise the undertaking he had received about his family, though it is not clear why he should have believed this promise from the unscrupulous gangsters with whom he was dealing, and who were virtually murdering him. Perhaps it was the only good element in an essentially tragic situation. If he was to die anyway, perhaps he wanted to die with some hope, and not bring all his family down with him in a final shoot-out in the house. Perhaps it was partly also his ingrained military obedience coming out even to the last.

At all events, Rommel then rejoined the waiting generals. They all climbed into the small green staff-car and drove off. They did not drive far. A few hundred yards up the hill from the Rommels' house, the car stopped in an open space at the edge of the wood. The driver and General Maisel got out and went for a walk. When they returned, five minutes later, General Burgdorf had left the car and was walking up and down the road beside it. Inside the car, Rommel lay on the back seat, 'lifeless' according to Maisel later, but still in his death-throes according to the driver. They sat him up, put his cap on his head and his Field Marshal's baton in his hand. They then drove off to the hospital at Ulm. It was from the hospital, about twenty minutes after Rommel had left his home, that the telephone rang there once again. Aldinger answered it, and took the message. 'The Field Marshal has had a haemorrhage, a brain storm, in the car. He is dead.'

It was officially stated that Rommel had died of his wounds. His state funeral was staged with great pomp four days later. It was a day of national mourning, ordered by Hitler. Four generals of the army stood at the four corners of the coffin, which lay in state, draped with an enormous swastika, in the town hall of Ulm. His decorations were laid out on a velvet cushion. The unfortunate von Runstedt, then the most senior officer in the German army, had to read Rommel's funeral oration in the name of the Führer. Read it he did, but he surely could not have written it too – not the old, embittered but always upstanding and patrician officer who never had anything but contempt for the Nazis. 'A pitiless destiny has snatched him from us, just at the moment when the fighting has come to its crisis', he said. Rommel had been a 'tireless fighter in the cause of the Führer and the Reich'; he had been 'imbued with the National Socialist spirit'. This was almost too much for von Runstedt, and the manner of his delivery became so stilted that when he ended with the words 'His heart belonged to the Führer', it was not only Frau Rommel in the congregation who longed to cry out that it was all a pack of lies.

Postscript

THERE ARE REALLY FOUR ASPECTS of Rommel: Rommel the military commander, Rommel the writer, Rommel the German and Rommel the creature of British imagination. Taking the last first, it is remarkable what an impact Rommel had on the British mind, quite unequalled by any other German commander during the war, after it or even today, thirty years later. One can, therefore, imagine his hold on the 8th Army in the desert war, and the urgent necessity of Auchinleck's message to his staffs in which he warned them of the danger of Rommel becoming some kind of 'magician or bogey man' and ordered them to 'dispel the idea that Rommel represented something more than an ordinary German general'. To the British, at the time – and not only to the Tommy – he clearly represented all that was reasonable in the German character, combined with a military genius and capacity for almost reckless success which seemed sadly lacking in British generals during the dim years of 1941 and 1942. How valid was this grudging kind of hero-worship, and how much was it an instinctive desire by all the British to build up the qualities of the man who was beating them – better after all to be conquered by a knight than by a knave? Auchinleck fell victim to the Rommel myth which he tried so hard to dispel by *diktat*, and then actually did dispel through his own actions. But in spite of what he achieved, there was obviously a deep British need to foster it, particularly in the political context of late 1942, when Great Britain so badly needed a success, and a big one at that. In a sense, the British were lucky to have an adversary who in reality conformed in so many respects to the image which they had created of him, which seems to have lasted intact when so many other wartime reputations have been undermined.

Rommel's calibre as a military commander has not only the two parts to it – Liddell Hart's 'conceptive and executive' – but also a third. The first two involve intellectual and practical qualities, but they could not prevail without a third, human quality – that of leadership. Rommel was not born a strategist. His conceptive powers grew in scale and in maturity very late in life, after his horizons widened. He started by thinking in terms of gullies and trenches, and ended by thinking in terms of continents. But, at all times, his strategy was more instinctive than analytical. If he had ruled Germany, instead of being merely one of her generals, he would probably – like Alexander the Great or the Swedish warrior kings – have led German legions into strategies of quite breathtaking extravagance. There would have been many victories; there would have been many defeats; above all there would have been continuous movement – continuous war – because Rommel's approach to warfare was based on an unbending faith in what the Germans called 'operations', which the British would call manœuvring.

The German army of Rommel's youth had been reared on the tradition that the Prussian victories of 1866 and 1870 had been won by the initiatives of the commanders on the spot, not those at Supreme Headquarters. This inspired a degree of delegation in 1914 which threatened to undermine the tight strategic control of the general staff, and there was then a reaction. When von Seeckt took over after the war, he attempted to restore the balance by retaining strategic control but encouraging a high degree of independent initiative in divisional commanders. Rommel was a direct inheritor of this tradition, and came naturally to the idea of manœuvring to exploit every fleeting opportunity – the 'strategy of expedients', as it had originally been called.

In fact, Rommel represented the triumph of the tactician over the strategist. However clearly he came to develop his own strategic view for Germany, he seemed continually to overlook the specifically tactical role which he was expected to play in the overall German plan, and to impute to the desert operations a much higher and more important position in German grand strategy than they were intended to have. His tactics in the desert – normally with inferior forces – were a mixture of brilliance and bluff, but they were always distinguished by lightfootedness, speed of reaction and an intuitive self-confidence which was conspicuously lacking in his opponents (and his allies). Of course, the difference

OPPOSITE Death mask of the hero of *Afrika*.

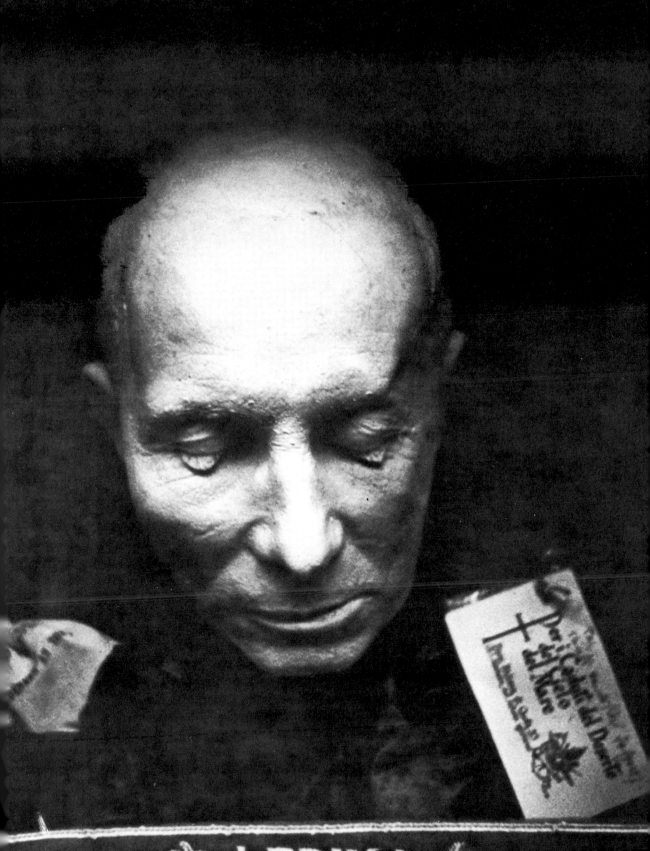

OPPOSITE On both sides, Rommel was one of the best known and admired generals of the entire war. The Rommel legend lives on: here James Mason plays the role of Rommel in the film *The Desert Fox*.

BELOW The film *The Desert Fox* recreates the tragic moment of Rommel's final leave-taking from his family.

between them, strategically, was that the British were putting their major effort into the desert, and so could not afford to lose it all, while the Germans were not.

Rommel's main impact on the war arose perhaps not so much from the results of his generalship as from the manner of it. More than any previous war, the Second World War epitomised the idea of total war in which nations deployed all their industrial and social as well as military resources, and in which communications ensured that the centre of decision remained for the most part in the capitals of the belligerents. Rommel did not seem to conform to this pattern. With him, the centre of decision was wherever he was. He restored to generalship the idea of leadership in battle from the front, regardless of the

increased mechanisation or scale and distance of operations. The desert made this easier, but it may be fair to suggest that – whatever Rommel's conceptive and executive talents – this manner of frontal command was feasible in modern war only at the divisional level, and perhaps it was at that level at which Rommel was at his best. The more senior he became, the less appropriate were these techniques of battlefield leadership, yet this whole approach to military command depended upon them. Above the level of the division, these additional factors would always cloud the luminous clarity of his tactical imagination. He certainly found discomfort in the inhibitions which arrived with greater responsibility. Politics and diplomacy were not his strong suits, but, instead of wilting under these new influences, he reacted violently against them, perhaps because he was subconsciously aware of his weakness in these fields and attempted to bury it by showing contempt for them.

Consequently his professional temperament appears, quite frankly, to have been rather unpleasant. He seemed unable to work with any equal or superior who disagreed with him. He wanted to make a clean sweep of what he called contemptuously the 'intellectual, academic' type of soldier on the general staff, and he allowed this contempt to warp his judgment in his dealings with the staff. Only Hitler seemed able to command any kind of obedience from him, and this again was a logical product of his earlier conditioning in the Kaiser's army. Rommel's subordinates knew better than to disagree with him – except in the thick of a battle, in which his prolonged absences sometimes made it unavoidable. To his subordinate generals, he tended to be equally as unpleasant as to his equals, but not to the rank and file. They knew him to be a plain enough man, who lived like them, worked as hard (indeed harder), fought as hard and who could lay out a platoon position as efficiently as he could plan a divisional attack.

As a military writer and thinker, Rommel matured beyond measure in the months of reflection after his return from Africa. The *Rommel Papers* are a monument to one of the most extraordinary military careers of the century. It was an extraordinary career because its significance was basically compressed into twenty-eight months of fighting – just over two years. Yet out of those twenty-eight months, Rommel has managed to create not only a narrative of brilliance but a series of post-mortems and treatises on warfare which have become classic military texts, and a sense of perspective of his desert

'Rommel's subordinates knew better than to disagree with him'

216

An heroic portrait of
Rommel, painted by Willrich
in 1942, as a souvenir
postcard among the Field
Marshal's huge popular
following in Germany.

command which remains almost unequalled by any other
literary commander of his seniority.

However, it was by looking at Rommel in the German context that this book began, and it is on the theme of Rommel as a
German that it ends; if only because he was a phenomenon
which it would be hard to find in any other twentieth-century
context than that of Germany. Where else could one find an
apparently rather dull, apolitical infantry officer rocketed from
Lieutenant-Colonel to Field Marshal in four years, and then
murdered by his masters after two more? As a German, his
apparent insensitivity to the German condition, to her political
circumstances, to her history, all have an unsatisfactory air.
There was a sort of dull, almost smug, patriotism about him,

which seemed to have no room for – and no need of – any further natural introspection. This could be attributed to an extreme narrowness of perspective, which was only just beginning to broaden when, as a Field Marshal at the age of fifty, he started to look over the parapet. Alternatively, it could be put down to an innocence and immaturity which was mitigated only when, again as a Field Marshal, he found himself forced into contact with experiences more general than those offered by the enclosed military world which he had inhabited until then. His background and development suggest that it was a bit of both.

Select Bibliography

Carver, Michael, *El Alamein*, Batsford, 1962

Carver, Michael, *Tobruk*, Batsford, 1964

Connell, John, *Auchinleck*, Cassell, 1959

Connell, John, *Wavell*, Collins, 1964

Görlitz, Walter, *The German General Staff*, Hollis & Carter, 1953

Liddell Hart, Capt. Sir Basil, *History of Second World War*, Cassell, 1970

Montgomery, F. M., Viscount of Alamein, *Memoirs*, Collins, 1958

Moorehead, Alan, *A Year of Battle*, Hamish Hamilton, 1943

Prittie, Terence, *Germans Against Hitler*, Hutchinson, 1964

Ritter, Gerhard, *The Sword and the Sceptre* (2 vols), Allen Lane, the Penguin Press, 1972

Rommel, Erwin, *Infantry Attacks*, translated by G. E. Kiddé, The Office of Alien Property, Justice Department, Washington, 1944

Rommel, Erwin, *The Rommel Papers* ed. B. H. Liddell Hart, Collins, 1953

Young, Brig. Desmond, *Rommel*, Collins, 1950

List of Illustrations

220

Index